Quarto.com

First published in 2017 by Voyageur Press, an imprint of The Quarto Group, 100 Cummings Center, Suite 265-D, Beverly, MA 01915, USA. T (978) 282-9590 F (978) 283-2742

Voyageur Press titles are also available at discount for retail, wholesale, promotional, and bulk purchase. For details, contact the Special Sales Manager by email at specialsales@quarto.com or by mail at The Quarto Group, Attn: Special Sales Manager, 100 Cummings Center, Suite 265-D, Beverly, MA 01915, USA.

ISBN: 978-0-7603-6859-6

Digital edition published in 2021
eISBN: 978-0-7603-6860-2

Originally found under the following Library of Congress Cataloging-in-Publication Data:

Names: Peterson, Chris, 1961- author.
Title: The pallet book : DIY projects for the home, garden, and homestead /
  by Chris Peterson.
Description: Minneapolis, Minnesota : Voyageur Press, 2018. | Includes index.
Identifiers: LCCN 2017017746 | ISBN 9780760352748 (pb)
Subjects: LCSH: Woodwork--Patterns. | Pallets (Shipping, storage, etc.) |
  Wood waste--Recycling.
Classification: LCC TT180 .P464 2018 | DDC 684/.08--dc23
LC record available at https://lccn.loc.gov/2017017746

Acquiring Editor: Thom O'Hearn
Project Manager: Jordan Wiklund
Design: Bad People Good Things LLC
Project Design: Chris Peterson
Photographer: Chris Marshall except pages 50-57, 61-63, 66-67, 73-75, 78-79, 92-95, 98-103, 110-111, 117-120, and 134-136 Crystal Liepa

THE NEW
PALLET
BOOK

INGENIOUS DIY PROJECTS FOR THE HOME, GARDEN, AND HOMESTEAD

CHRIS PETERSON

COOL
SPRINGS
PRESS

CONTENTS

INTRODUCTION

The popularity of the maker movement, the upcycling of existing resources, and the homesteading trend all show no signs of abating. That's because all three only make common sense—especially for money-conscious individuals. Reuse something like a pallet and you've not only made the most of a free asset, but you've also kept one more item out of the waste stream, doing your part to clean up our increasingly polluted lands. Let's be honest, though: The bigger draw is the unbridled satisfaction of crafting something useful and even attractive with your own hands and ingenuity, for less than the cost of a couple lattes.

That is a unique reward, available to the home DIYer willing to put in a few hours and some honest effort. The reality is, most home craftspeople actually find that time well spent, fun, and a great creative outlet. As exercises in imagination go, you'd be hard-pressed to find a better palette for your creative inspiration than a, well, pallet. This new edition of *The Pallet Book* helps you do that more effectively than ever before. Peruse this updated version and you'll discover new and exciting projects and explore different techniques that you can, in turn, use to design and craft your own flights of fancy using the medium of

pallets. Ultimately, it's a way to exploit a nearly limitless resource.

Wood pallets are ubiquitous. You probably don't even realize how often you see them because they are so very commonplace. That's because they are used to transport goods small and large. From one end of the country to the other, there are trucks driving along the highway at this very moment with their trailers chock-full of pallets carrying the next load of car tires, printers, or cooking oil. Almost everything that goes into a store and out the front door arrives by way

This incredibly sophisticated and detailed seating area was built using whole and deconstructed pallets. The result speaks for itself . . . and the versatility of pallets.

Pallets really shine when used for indoor furnishings. As this large, contemporary coffee table shows, they provide a wholly unique look that can bridge the divide between rough-hewn industrial and simply chic.

Why pay the high prices for durable, fun, comfortable patio furniture when you can make your own from pallets? These chunky Adirondack chairs are colorful examples of the type of long-lasting and handsome outdoor seating you achieve with a few recycled pallets and a quart or two of paint.

The enterprising homesteader can use pallets to create entire outbuildings quickly, easily, and inexpensively. This storage barn is a perfect example, assembled from nothing more than pallets, nails, and tar paper.

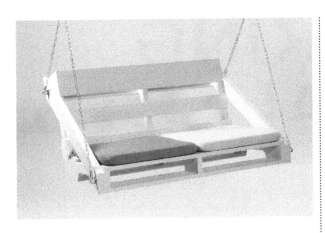

of a pallet. Because it's often easier and not terribly expensive to use new pallets rather than reuse old, shipping companies create a stream of thousands of extra pallets just lying around waiting to be reused. Those represent a treasure trove of potential for the enterprising home craftsperson.

There are basically two ways this incredible resource is given new life. The first is to reuse the pallet, all or mostly intact, to create a new structure. This is how people build fences with pallets, and how projects such as the Platform Bed (page 106) and Porch Swing (page 33) are crafted. The main attraction to larger projects such as these—aside from the sheer usefulness of the furniture or finished goods—is that it takes less work to fabricate a project that calls for little or no pallet disassembly. The second type of reuse is to pull apart the pallets to one degree or another and repurpose the sturdy wood into new and innovative creations. This type of project offers a wider range or potential uses, from the utilitarian beauty of a Clock (page 132) to the classic comfort of an Adirondack Chair (page 45).

The big variable here will be the pallets you use. As is the case with so much in our world, older versions were built sturdier and with older growth—often hardwood—boards. Today, many pallets are built to be disposable, with flawed lumber sometimes irregularly cut. As you'll read in chapter 1, pallet sizes vary, so you need to avoid ever assuming the measurements of any given board used in a pallet. That makes acquiring free pallets to recycle even more important—you'll be more willing to discard pieces and make more extensive changes if you didn't pay for the wood source.

Regardless of which level of deconstruction the project you choose requires, or the particular pallet you have at your disposal, the steps in these projects are not backbreaking and certainly not technically demanding. In fact, one of the great things about using pallets to build your projects is how simple and easy they are to work with. The shape and size of pallet lumber is naturally adaptable to a stunning number of new uses. Those boards are also easy to square and cut to integrate into completely novel applications.

That all means that the projects in the pages that follow are fairly easy and quick to build. You won't need a fully equipped woodworking workshop or a veteran woodworker's knowledge to tackle any of these. All the tools and techniques are just about as basic as can be. Simple, time-tested general rules like "measure twice, cut once" will serve you well. Beyond that, it's just a matter of putting in a modest amount of time and effort for a result you'll be proud to show off.

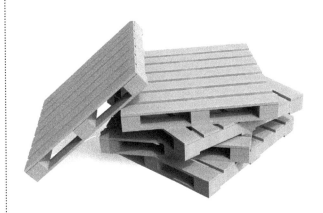

CHAPTER ONE

WORKING WITH PALLETS

The more you learn about pallets, the more you'll discover the pure beauty in their simplicity. Not only does the basic form lend itself to being used wholesale in a number of creative applications, but pallet construction also ensures that these incredibly useful items can easily be taken apart and incorporated into new creations that are far more than the sum of their pallet parts. This chapter offers a brief primer that provides everything you need to know to master working with the ever-adaptable pallet.

Stringer Pallet

THE ANATOMY OF THE PALLET

The basic difference among pallets is the way in which forklift blades slide under the pallet. A pallet can be designed as "two-way," accessible from only two opposite sides, or "four-way," accessible from any direction. Obviously, this affects how the pallet can be used. To complicate matters, there are partial four-way pallets with cutouts in the side stringers (the sturdier boards that support the deck boards and run perpendicular to them). These pallets are meant to be lifted or skidded from the front or back, or lifted from the sides.

Different manufacturers produce vastly different sizes, shapes, and qualities of pallets. The most common are forty by forty-eight inches with two-by-four stringers and one deck board. But that's just a baseline. End, or "lead," boards are often wider—five and a half inches rather than three and a half inches—and the spacing between boards varies. Beyond that, there are more than half a dozen sizes used for different purposes, and construction in any case is far from precise. Today's manufacturers are far more likely than in the past to use especially thin and hard-to-work-with deck boards ready to adapt to the pallets with which you're working.

Different manufacturers use different widths and thicknesses of deck boards. The most common are one-by-fours, or an actual size of three-quarters inch by three and a half inches. End or "lead" deck boards are often wider, such as one-by-sixes (actual size of three-quarters inch by five and a half inches). In reality, pallet construction is not overly precise. Manufacturers can use unsightly wood that wouldn't be marketable as boards. There is also a lot of variance in the different pieces. Although stringers are usually standard sizes, depending on where you find the pallet and who manufactured it, deck boards can range in thickness from three-eighths inch to three-quarters inch. That means that you may have to adapt the projects in this book to the thickness of deck board on the pallets you salvage.

Block Pallet

Pallets are also available in a range of overall dimensions. The most common in the United States is forty-eight inches by forty inches, but different industries use different size pallets to ship material and equipment specific to a given industry. There are also smaller units meant to ship smaller loads or to be used in smaller delivery trucks or vehicles.

International pallets add even more sizes into the mix, not only because they're using metric measurements, but because European trucks and shipping containers are often sized to much different dimensions than American vehicles.

All these variables mean that you need to keep an open mind when reclaiming pallets. The units you find for reuse may well be far from "standard," but that doesn't make them less usable. The pallets specified in all the projects in this book are standard stringer pallets with nominal two-by-four stringers, and nominal one-by-four decking; we assume an overall width of forty-eight inches by forty inches. We have used "notched" stringer pallets (partial four-way) for many of these, because they are some of the most commonly available types of pallets. The notch can make for an interesting appearance, depending on where it falls in the span of the cut piece. However, the notches can also present design and structural challenges, depending on what you're building. Where there might be structural concerns—such as a weight-bearing leg—we've turned to "unnotched" two-way stringers.

That said, all these projects have been developed for maximum adaptability, to allow you to customize the plans to whatever pallets you may have reclaimed.

OTHER PALLET TYPES

The pallet formats shown here are the most common. However, there are other formats. Most any wood pallet can be adapted for use in the projects in this book.

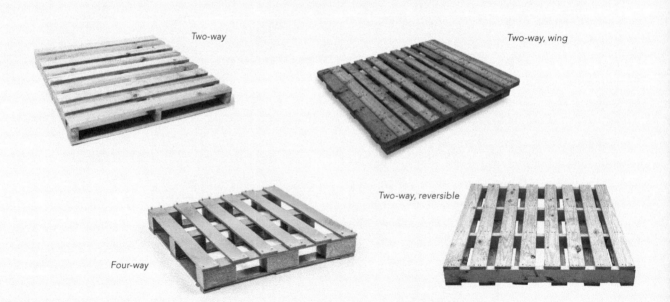

Two-way

Two-way, wing

Two-way, reversible

Four-way

COMMON US PALLET SIZES

SIZE	USE
48 × 40	General, grocery store
42 × 42	Paint, wire spools
48 × 48	Metal drums
48 × 42	Chemicals, beverage industry
40 × 40	Dairy products
48 × 20	General retail
36 × 36	Beverage
48 × 45	Automotive parts

COMMON INTERNATIONAL PALLET SIZES

SIZE	CONTINENT
39.37 × 47.24	Europe, Asia
44.88 × 44.88	Australia
43.30 × 43.30	Asia
31.50 × 47.24	Europe

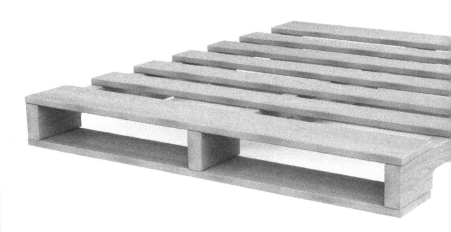

A standard "partial four-way" stringer pallet. Note the notches in the side stringer that allow for forklift blades but still provide a surface for a limited number of bottom deck boards.

Pallets of all kinds can be used to make furnishings and accents that are limited only by imagination. Here, block pallets have been chopped up and reassembled to make a chunky, rustic living room sofa and coffee table. They may not be the height of luxury, but they are durable, usable, and basically free!

Uniformly colored pallets like these should be avoided. The color is usually a sign that the pallet was used to ship a particular material, often chemicals or other potentially toxic substances.

THE HUNT FOR PALLETS

It's not hard to find pallets for reclamation because they're used to ship so many materials and products. The trick is to locate pallets that are in fairly decent shape and that aren't spoken for. Although the easiest places to find a wealth of pallets are behind big-box stores and large retailers where they may be stacked haphazardly, many of these companies have agreements with recyclers to bulk collect used pallets. (Remember, pallets in good shape can be reused again and again.)

Unless the pallets have obviously been discarded as trash—on the curb during large trash pickup day or in a local dump—you'll need to ask permission to take them. That said, many companies are more than willing to have you cart them off. That includes construction companies on large construction sites,

where they often don't have anywhere to store pallets to keep them out of the path of workers and vehicles, and they may not have arranged to have the pallets removed. You may also get lucky and find whole dumpsters full of unbroken or slightly damaged pallets.

Regardless of where you find them, you'll want to make absolutely sure that the pallets you reclaim are safe for reuse. This involves determining if they have been used to transport any toxic or dangerous materials and avoiding those that have. Fortunately, most pallets are marked on the top, bottom, or sides, and the markings often tell the story of where the pallet came from and what it carried.

COMMON PALLET MARKINGS

IPPC [a]: This is the mark of the International Plant Protection Convention and certifies that the wood used in the pallet does not contain invasive plant or insect species. IPPC pallets must be treated to kill any organisms remaining in the wood—either through debarking or heat treatment.

DB [b]: The pallet has been debarked, but is otherwise untreated. Generally safe for projects.

HT [b]: Heat treating pallets kills organisms that might have survived milling, rendering the pallet safe for use—especially in projects.

KD [b]: This means the wood was kiln dried. For the purposes of an upcycling project, it's the same as heat treating. Kiln drying also ensures that the wood will be less likely to warp or deform when you reuse it.

MB [b]: The pallet has been treated with methyl bromide and should be avoided for upcycling.

EPAL: This is the European Pallet Association logo; it certifies that the pallet has been debarked and heat treated, and verifies that the wood is safe to use in projects.

EUR: This predates the current European Pallet Association designation, and you cannot reliably be sure of which chemicals may have been used on the pallet. Many upcyclers avoid pallets with this mark.

PRL: This stamp proves verification by the Packaging Research Laboratory, indicating that the pallet has been treated with high-temperature heat treatment and does not contain toxic chemicals. This is a good sign for anyone looking to upcycle the pallet.

Colored pallets: Pallets that are uniformly colored all over with red, blue, or brown are used by specific industries such as pool and spa manufacturers. These have likely been exposed to toxic chemicals and are subsequently not used for upcycling.

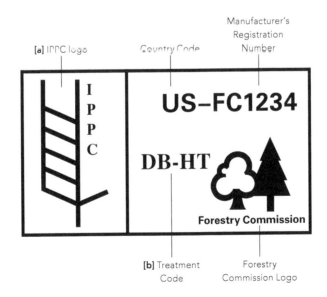

[a] IPPC logo Country Code Manufacturer's Registration Number

US–FC1234

DB-HT Forestry Commission

[b] Treatment Code Forestry Commission Logo

DECONSTRUCTING PALLETS

Once you've laid your hands on some safe and structurally sound pallets, you'll probably need to modify them for whatever purpose you have in mind. Although several of the projects in this book make use of whole pallets, you'll often need to deconstruct a pallet to one degree or another for upcycling.

When it comes to taking pallets apart, the right tools will save you time, money, and effort, and can even prevent injury. The job is not necessarily as easy as it might appear, because pallet manufacturers use very stubborn fasteners, such as shank nails, and trying to separate the pieces can lead to the destruction of much usable wood. Often, the best way to remove deck boards from stringers or blocks is to actually cut the nails. Occasionally you'll be faced with sacrificing a section of wood that simply can't be separated from another section. In any case, here's a list of basic deconstruction tools that are also used to craft many of the projects in the book.

Hammer. A basic claw hammer is the crudest and least effective method to separate pallet boards. Even using a wedge to help pry a board up, the hammer will often destroy the end of a board rather than budge the fasteners.

Wood or polyurethane mallet. Sometimes getting a deck board loose of its connection to a stringer is a matter of finesse and using a soft touch rather than brute force. A wood or polyurethane mallet can slowly but surely free a board without causing much damage to the board's face.

Pry bar. A good pry bar can give you just the right amount of leverage exactly where you need it to loosen stubborn boards, but using a pry bar to take apart a pallet requires patience and a great deal of effort. It can also lead to breakage and, specifically, end splitting.

Pallet buster. Pallet busters are specially constructed to exert maximum force on the fasteners without cracking boards. The long handle and shaped tines use physics to require a minimum of effort for a maximum of force. The downside is that these tools tend to be pricey. Consequently, it only makes sense to purchase one if you plan on breaking down quite a few pallets.

Reciprocating saw. Known commonly by the brand name Sawzall, this hardworking saw can tear through stringers, blocks, and boards alike, as if they were butter. Equipped with a metal-cutting blade, the saw can cut between boards and stringers, severing stubborn fasteners. When the board can't be removed, or a thick stringer needs to be cut to size, a reciprocating saw is sometimes the best option.

Circular saw. If you simply can't loosen the fasteners or get at them with a reciprocating saw—or if the board is already damaged—a circular saw will be your best friend. This tool can be indispensible in quickly and accurately cutting deck boards free of overly nailed ends. Adding a fine-tooth finish blade will ensure you make the clean cuts necessary for some of the more delicate and exacting projects in this book.

Handsaw. Never underestimate the control and potential of a good, sharp, crosscut or combination handsaw. Although it will take more time and effort than a circular saw, this might be a more effective, efficient option for single cuts and those where a circular saw might be the wrong size.

Nippers. This handy tool is essentially a specialized pair of pliers, effective at pulling nails or, in the case of pallets, nail fragments or cut ends out of wood meant for upcycling projects.

Frameless hacksaw. If you don't want to invest in or use a reciprocating saw, this handy little tool can be a great alternative. It is basically a handle that holds a metal-cutting blade. The blade projects straight out from the handle, so there is no "frame" to get in the way of intricate or awkward cuts. The blade is thin enough to slip in between a deck board and the edge of a stringer to cut a nail. It will take more time and effort than a reciprocating saw would, but it can often go places the power tool can't and is safer and cheaper to use.

When deconstructing pallets, it's often wisest to start with the simplest solution and work up from there. If the pallet is not constructed with special nails, a hammer may do the trick. But most pallets are going to require a more involved solution.

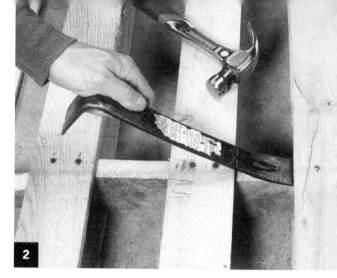

HOW TO DECONSTRUCT A PALLET: FOUR OPTIONS

1. Where the board ends are already loose or standard nails have been used, a claw hammer can work to separate a deck board. Use another hammer or mallet to secure the claw end under the end of the board as close to the nails as possible, and then carefully lever the board up.

2. Pry bars have an advantage over claw hammers in their shape. The wide face and gentle curve of the handle combine to spread stress over a wider area, which means less board breakage.

Tap the tongue of the bar under one side of the board near the nails and slowly lever the board up a tiny bit. Then work on the other side of the board. Repeat until the board end breaks loose.

3. To use a pallet buster, simply wedge the tines under the board and lever up even firmly attached boards with ease and a minimum of breakage. However, these justify their cost only when you're deconstructing several pallets.

4. When other options aren't going to do the trick, slide the moving metal-cutting blade of a reciprocating saw between a board and the stringer or block, quickly severing any fasteners.

FINISHING TOUCHES

Although several of the projects shown in this book can be left unfinished, many should be finished. Depending on the pallets you're upcycling, the wood may be distressed, presenting splinters and an unpleasant surface to the touch. Some are so rough that you may have to simply accept a more rustic appearance or the fact that you can't smooth them down enough to take a gloss layer of paint. Remember, design flexibility is key when upcycling pallet wood.

A jointer is an effective way to square up pallet boards, giving them clean, sharp edges and flat faces that mate perfectly in projects like the ones in this book. However, a jointer is a fairly expensive piece of woodworking machinery and not every shop has one. In addition, a jointer only works on fairly thick pieces. If you have deconstructed deck boards thinner than three-quarters of an inch, jointing them may not be an option.

Even if you don't have access to a jointer, you can square off the faces of pallet boards with defects using a table saw; it will just take more careful handling. In either case, you'll need to adjust measurements, because in removing wood to square up members, you'll be altering the actual dimensions of the pieces.

Sanding is the solution for any project where you want smoother edges on your pallet.

A simple sanding can clean up modest defects, except where the wood is so substandard as to be unworkable. If you're finishing the project, sand the project as part of prep. You can use an old-fashioned sanding block and sheets of sandpaper, but the more efficient solution is a palm sander. These can smooth pallet-wood surfaces quickly and give you far more control than belt or orbital sanders.

SAFETY FIRST

When working with wood taken from a pallet, be careful that there are no hidden fasteners that might cause damage to a saw or injury to the user. Staples, portions of a nail, or other errant pieces of metal can be a danger when working with reclaimed wood. Ensure that the wood you use is free of these by using a lumber metal detector. These handy devices are simple wands that work much like a stud finder; just wave them over the wood and they alert you to any metal—even hidden small pieces of nails.

FINE FINISHES

Prepping and finishing pallet wood can be your way of giving any pallet-wood project a polished look. It's also your chance to ensure an upscale project gives no clues to its original identity. Just know that some wood you salvage from pallets may not take a finish because of an overly rough or degraded surface. The challenge is that there isn't just one type of pallet wood. Different manufacturers use different woods. In fact, the same manufacturer may use different woods at different times, depending on availability. Different woods take paint or stains differently (which is why it's always good to do a practice run on a scrap piece of the wood you intend to finish).

Adding to the jumble, different pallets will be rougher or smoother, depending on how and where they were manufactured. They will also be less or more dirty, depending on how old the pallet is and what it was used to carry. That's why preparation is key, no matter what final look you're after.

PREPPING PALLET WOOD

Prepping the wood you've reclaimed from a pallet starts with cleaning. If, in the fabrication process, you already smoothed the edges and faces of the boards, chances are that they won't need to be cleaned. However, if the wood came from a well-traveled pallet that you simply disassembled (or used mostly whole), it may need to be cleaned prior to sanding and prepping.

Soap and water may do the trick for superficial dirt and even mild grease marks. More stubborn stains and grease can be removed with trisodium phosphate (TSP), following the manufacturer's instructions on the box. No matter how you clean the wood, make sure it's absolutely dry before you continue prepping it. Most finishes require a sanded surface with just enough tooth to allow the finish to absorb into the surface. For pallet wood, that generally means working down from 80-grit to 110- or 120-grit sandpaper. Depending on the size of the project, sand by hand or use a palm sander. Think twice before turning to a belt or orbital sander. Given the mottled shades of some pallet wood, it's easy with these more powerful tools to spend too long on one spot and sand a slope or depression into the surface. This can be a critical error on thinner deck boards, where it can weaken the board beyond use.

If you're planning on using a high-gloss product to finish your project, follow up any sanding with a wipe-down using a slightly damp, lint-free cloth or tack cloth. Even minute particles of dust can ruin a smooth, glossy surface.

A FLAWLESS FINISH

Painting a pallet-wood project isn't much different than painting any other type of wood. Use a quality primer to lay down a good bed for the topcoat. The best brush to use to paint most of the projects in this book is a two-inch chip brush. For flawless gloss surfaces, sand lightly between coats (you can add up to four coats).

If you're staining a project, consider using a stain-and-sealant product to cut down on the work you'll need to do. These formulations offer great coverage and an all-in-one solution. However, whether you're staining or finishing with a combination product, it's wise to test the product on the underside of a board or other inconspicuous area. For the same reason, it's always good to start with a light coat, because it's much easier to darken a stain than it is to lighten it.

For the outdoor projects in this book, a sealant topcoat, such as polyurethane or spar varnish, is a good idea to ensure the longevity of what you build. However, keep in mind that pallet wood was meant for exposure to abuse and the elements, so even unfinished, the wood will usually hold up for a long time.

SPECIAL EFFECTS

If you're after a weathered, aged look with a painted project, skip the primer and let the paint soak into the wood unevenly. You can also lightly sand areas of the wood to erode portions of the paint. As an alternative, use multiple paint colors, sanding away the topcoat to reveal patches of the color underneath. To distress a surface you'll be staining, beat it lightly with a chain or other implement to create the appearance of timeworn damage. Then stain as you would otherwise.

CHAPTER TWO

OUTDOOR EYE-CATCHERS

Start with this fact: Pallets are incredibly rugged. They spend a great deal of time outdoors, exposed to the elements, dirt, and rough handling. That makes them ideal as the foundation for interesting, useful, and even fun outdoor projects.

Use pallet wood for a main feature in your backyard and you won't have to worry about finishing it or keeping pets or pool water at bay. The wood will take your worst and keep on looking great. However, because it is so good at taking both stain and paint, outdoor pallet creations are a great way to spruce up the look of a patio, yard, grassy incline, or any gathering space under the sun and the stars.

You'll find a full range of projects in this chapter, including those that require a great deal of construction and offer the reward of a very useful, value-added feature. (Lazy Porch Swing anyone? You'll find it on page 33.) Creating outdoor furniture is one of the most common upcycle uses for the pallets, and one of the reasons why is that the furniture is somewhat forgiving of less-than-exact tolerances that are often the product of using pallets. That doesn't mean you have to dive into building a Chaise Lounge (page 37); you can just as easily and happily start with something simple and fun, like a Toss Across Game Board (page 61) or a Pool Noodle and Towel Rack (page 66). The choice, as always, is yours. So is the enjoyment and satisfaction of furnishing your backyard with a cool, unique look for next to nothing.

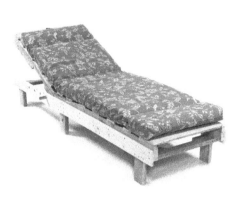

SMALL-BIRD BIRDHOUSE

WHAT YOU'LL NEED

TOOLS:
Circular saw • Speed square • Measuring tape • Hole saw with 1 ¼" bit • Bar clamps • Power drill and bits • 2 ½" paintbrush (optional)

MATERIALS:
1 pallet • 100-grit sandpaper • Wood glue • Finish nails • Wood putty • Paint (optional) • Eye screws • Small-gauge chain or paracord

TIME: 20 MINUTES **DIFFICULTY:** EASY

Unless you have musician neighbors, the prettiest sound you'll hear in your backyard is the call of song-birds. Of course, that means you have to invite them into the yard in the first place, and there's no better invitation than a short-term rental your feathered friends can call their own.

The challenge is that small songbirds will only stay in a residence where they feel safe. If the entry hole and space inside are too large, the songbirds will quickly be evicted by larger, more aggressive birds. And, unfortunately, crows and blue jays aren't known for the pretty sounds they make. That's why this house is sized just right for birds such as starlings or sparrows. Pair the house with a squirrel-proof bird feeder and you may even get songbirds to overwinter in the residence.

The design is fairly plain, but you can spruce it up with paint or decorations to match the look of your yard or garden. Birds won't be put off by unusual color schemes. Just make sure to hang the birdhouse where predators such as cats can't get to it, or the birds will head to more welcoming pastures. In any case, plan on disassembling the birdhouse after a few seasons to clean it out and keep your bird visitors safe from parasites and diseases.

The construction itself is basic and translates to a super-easy woodworking project. Even if your skill level is firmly in the "beginner" camp, you'll find this birdhouse doable. Just keep in mind that a small project such as this is not forgiving of errors; be precise and careful with your measurements and you'll wind up with a yard accent that does justice to the birds and the landscaping in equal measure.

HOW YOU MAKE IT

1. Use the circular saw to cut 1 x 6" end deck boards into two sidewalls 8 ½" long; a floor 4" long; and front and back walls 11" long. Use a speed square to mark two 45° cuts in one end of each wall to create a peak. Cut the roof pieces 10" long, and rip one down to 4 ¾" wide.

2. Use a 1 ¼" hole saw to drill the entry hole in the front wall, 8" up from the bottom and centered side to side.

3. Sand the pieces with 100-grit sandpaper. Make sure the entry hole is smooth.

4. Clamp the floor of the birdhouse to a worktable and align a sidewall in position along one long edge, with the edges flush. Drill pilot holes through the base. Coat the edge of the floor with wood glue and nail the wall to the floor with finish nails. Repeat with the opposite wall.

5. Attach the front and back walls in the same way, edge-gluing the surfaces to one another and drilling pilot holes for the finish nails along the edges.

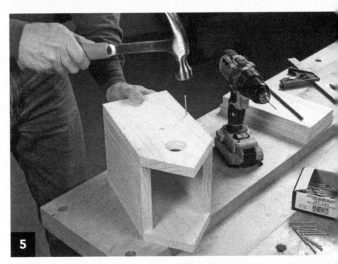

6. Clamp the shorter roof surface to the worktable and align the longer one along the edge. Drill pilot holes, coat the mating edges with wood glue, and nail the roof together.

7. Set the roof in place on the birdhouse body, centered front to back. Drill pilot holes every 2" along the front and back edges. Coat the mating edges with glue and nail the roof to the walls.

8. Putty over nailheads, sand, and paint as desired. Screw in two eye screws opposite each other on either side of the roof. Hang the birdhouse from a tree limb with small-gauge chain or paracord.

CUSTOMIZING YOUR BIRDHOUSE

This project includes some features that may not be advisable, depending on how you want to use your birdhouse and what birds you're hoping to attract. If you want to guarantee the longevity of your birdhouse, you may want to substitute galvanized screws for the finish nails used here. The birdhouse also makes use of a one-and-one-quarter-inch entry hole, but some birds prefer different size holes. The chart below provides measurements for common birds you may be looking to attract.

BIRD	HOLE SIZE	PLACEMENT HEIGHT FROM GROUND
Eastern Bluebird	1½"	8' high, in open area
Tree Swallow	1"	6-8' high, in open area
Purple Martin	2⅛"	20' high
Tufted Titmouse	1¼"	8-10' high
Chickadee	1⅛"	6-8' high
Nuthatch	1¼"	20-25' high
Wren	1"	8-10' high

Also be aware that placement of the house will affect whether birds will use it. Aside from the height recommended above, keep birdhouses away from thick shrubs or branch growth that could serve as concealment of access to the birdhouse for a predator such as a cat. It's ideal to maintain a clear line of sight around the birdhouse, wherever it is hung or mounted on a post, wall, or tree.

SMALL PLANTER

WHAT YOU'LL NEED

TOOLS:
Circular saw or table saw • Measuring tape • Metal framing square • Power drill and bits • Staple gun • Palm sander or sanding block • Paintbrush (optional)

MATERIALS:
2 pallets • 2" nails • 3" wood screws • Landscape fabric • 2" wood screws • 80-grit sandpaper • Wood putty • Paint or finish (optional) • Tools

TIME: 30 MINUTES   **DIFFICULTY:** EASY

A standalone planter is one of the most useful additions to any yard, garden, deck, or patio. The portability of a planter such as this one means you can move sensitive trees or shrubs inside or out, depending on the weather. It also allows you to give the plant exactly the amount of sun it needs, or put edible container plants where they'll be most accessible.

Although this is a small planter, it will accommodate many different plants, from a rhododendron to a miniature rosebush to a tree such as a crepe myrtle. One of the wonderful things about planter culture is that you control watering and soil, so you can plant your ornamental in the richest, most nutritious loam possible, with just the right acid balance to keep it healthy and thriving. The control over environment also means you can adjust the soil to grow fussy, high-maintenance plants that might otherwise be impossible to nurture in your garden.

The planter itself is easy to build. The design is entirely scalable and straightforward, with a minimum of cutting and fabrication. You can customize the look with different color paints (don't paint or finish the interior), stains, or clear finishes. If you decide to paint the planter in a color, make sure the hue you've chosen blends well with the house and landscaping, or the look will grow old and dated very quickly. In most cases, it's usually best to leave the planter unfinished.

You can, however, dress up your planter in other ways. Simple stencils are a great decoration that adds visual interest to the planter. Metal straps can also create a distinctive look. For instance, line the top or bottom trim—or both—with copper bands. The copper will age into a fetching matte green patina that blends seamlessly with the look of the wood.

HOW YOU MAKE IT

1. Cut eight side panels 20" long and eight side panels 17 ½" long, from deck boards. Cut eight corner trim pieces 16" long, from deck boards.

2. Assemble the planter side panels on a flat, level work surface. Align two trim pieces, vertical and parallel, spaced about 12" apart. Stack four panels of the same length in a column, face down on the trim pieces. The top edge of the top panel should be flush to the top of the trim pieces. Use a framing square to check that the panels are perfectly aligned.

3. Adjust the trim pieces so that they protrude exactly the width of one of your deck boards on each side (use a scrap piece of deck board as a spacer). Nail the panels to the trim with two nails per end.

4. Repeat the process to build the remaining walls. Position one short wall against the inside edge of one long wall to create one corner of the planter. Drill four pilot holes spaced evenly down each trim piece and screw the panels together with 3" wood screws. Repeat with the remaining walls to construct the box of the planter.

5. Measure the exact width of the bottom at three places along the inside of the box (it should be 17 ½"). Cut the bottom boards from stringers to fit. Screw the four floorboards in place, spaced evenly, with 3" wood screws. Drill ⅛" holes in a random pattern in the floorboards, for drainage.

6. Line the inside of the box with landscape fabric, cut and doubled over as necessary, and stapled to the walls. The fabric should create a tight pocket for the dirt.

7. Cut the top frame pieces 23" long, from deck boards. Miter the ends 45°, and dry fit the frame to the top of the box. Drill pilot holes down into the trim and walls, and attach the frame with 2" wood screws. (If the deck boards you're using are less than ¾" thick, you may need to use 1 × 1" cleats—cut from stringer waste material—to create a holding surface for the top frame.)

8. Cover the screwheads with wood putty, let dry, and sand the planter smooth. Paint or finish the planter as desired. Position the planter in its final location. Fill it with potting soil and your preferred plant.

PLANTER BOX PARTNERS

Sure, it can be just a simple home for a plant, but this planter can also be paired with a number of structures to make the most of its potential. These include add-ons that serve a purely aesthetic purpose and more useful complements that increase the types of plants you can grow. Choose the one that makes the most sense for your garden and preferences.

● **THE UNPLANTED PLANTER.** You don't necessarily have to go to the trouble of lining and planting the planter. You can opt for the quick-switch option of seasonal flowering plants or plants already at home in a container by simply placing the container in the planter. For short pots and other shallow containers, place bolsters made from scraps of pallet wood under the pot so that the top of the lip sits about even with the top of the planter (make sure the drainage holes in the container are not blocked). If you want to maintain the illusion of a planted planter, top the container with tufts of peat or coir, and fill the spaces between the container and the inside surfaces of the planter with the material.

● **THE PLANTER COLD FRAME.** Cold frames are popular for avid gardeners who want to keep their edible gardens growing into the winter. You can use the same idea with this planter. Remove the soil halfway down the planter and plant it with lettuces, herbs, or other low-growing edibles. Add a simple thermometer inside, right above the soil. Then, when the cold weather hits, cover the top with an old window, a sheet of Plexiglas, or even a sheet of six-mil plastic sheeting held in place with rocks or bricks around the lip of the planter. If you're feeling ambitious, you can build a simple frame from pallet-wood scraps to hold the window material. Either way, keep an eye on the growing edibles, because the cold frame will most likely need to be vented as the temperature rises in the direct midday sun, to keep the plants from wilting.

● **TRELLISED TO IMPRESS.** A trellis can be a beautiful complement to a wood planter—one that opens up the type and species of plants you can grow. A simple trellis attached to one side of the planter will support climbing or sprawling plants and can create a green wall. For even more impressive eye candy, install a corner trellis, and tuck the planter into the inside corner of a house or patio.

PATIO LOVESEAT

WHAT YOU'LL NEED

TOOLS:
Pry bar or hammer • Power drill and bits • Circular saw or reciprocating saw • Speed square • Pencil • Palm sander • Paintbrush (optional) • Bar clamps

MATERIALS:
4 pallets • 6" wood screws • 6" lag screws • 1 ½" wood screws • 2" finish nails • 4" lag screws • 100-grit sandpaper • Seat and back cushions (optional) • Paint, stain, or other finish (optional)

TIME: 1 HOUR **DIFFICULTY:** MEDIUM

Let's face it; patio furniture is downright expensive. Even cheap plastic versions aren't all that cheap. The investment is even more galling when you consider how short the life span of patio furniture can be, given relentless exposure to bright sunlight and the elements.

The answer? Build your own nearly free outdoor seating.

Although it might not be the first option that pops to mind, pallet wood is a fantastic material for creating extremely durable, comfortable, and low-cost outdoor furnishings. Think about it. Not only do you want your patio furniture to hold up to day after day of harsh sunlight, but it also needs to tolerate the occasional downpour. Of course, it also has to handle the rough-and-tumble of a neighborhood cookout or kids and pets having fun outside. Build patio or deck furnishings out of pallets, and you're using wood that was originally selected for its incredible strength, resilience, and durability.

This loveseat is a perfect example of the kind of extraordinary outdoor fixture pallets can become. It will endure not only the elements but also food and drink spills as well as rambunctious relatives and youngsters. It's small enough to fit even a tiny townhouse patio and comfortable enough to spend hours in.

This is such a cozy seating option that you may want to pair it with the Adirondack Chair (see page 45) to create a seating group around a fire pit. With fun, handsome, and durable seating like this waiting outside your backdoor, you may even find yourself spending more time outside the house than in it.

HOW YOU MAKE IT

1. Remove the deck boards from the bottom of a pallet. Set the pallet on a clean, flat, level work surface (the ends of the stringers will be pointing to the front). Set another pallet on top. The stringers should be aligned and the pallets should be flush side to side and front to back. Stringer notches, if any, should all be facing down.

2. Bar-clamp the panels. Screw the pallets together by driving 4" wood screws down at an angle through the ends of the top stringers and into the top edges of the stringers below. Screw the end deck boards together with 1 ½" wood screws, using four per side.

3. Remove one end deck board from the top of a third pallet. Place it on top of the two base pallets. Screw it to the pallet below, in the same way you joined the lower two pallets.

4. Nail two deck boards across the front ends of the stringers with 2" finish nails, to form a fascia on the front of the loveseat.

5. Remove the deck boards from the bottom of a pallet. Cut the stringers 25" long, removing a top deck board as necessary to make the cut. This will form the back of the loveseat. Use a speed square and pencil to mark a 15° angle on the face of each stringer at the cut end. Use a circular saw to make the angle cuts.

6. Enlist a helper to place the seatback in position, with the cut stringer ends sitting flush on the exposed stringers of the top pallet. Drill angled holes through the edges of the back's stringers, down into the top of the seat stringers. Countersink the holes and fasten the back to the top seat pallet with 6" lag screws.

7. Sand the loveseat all over. Remove any splinters and smooth any rough sections. Paint or stain the loveseat if desired, or leave it natural to blend with the landscaping. Make the loveseat more comfortable by adding seat and back cushions.

CREATIVE OPTIONS FOR PATIO LOVESEATS

Although the design of the patio loveseat is meant to be both compact and attractive, you can customize your loveseat to better suit the dimensions and features of your yard.

● **CONVERT TO PERIMETER SEATING FOR SMALL YARDS.** Remove the back from this loveseat and the base can be attached directly to fencing around the outside of a small yard, to take up the smallest footprint while still offering plenty of seating. Screw the base directly to wood or plastic fencing; drill holes in the base and wire it to cyclone or steel wire fencing.

● **EXPLOIT LARGE OUTDOOR AREAS BY USING MULTIPLES OF THE LOVESEAT.** This design doesn't include arms, which makes it easy to join multiple loveseats into a large seating structure that might work better in a long narrow yard or just to border one edge of a large patio or deck.

● **GO POOLSIDE BY LOWERING THE LOVESEAT.** Omit the bottom layer of pallets for the seat to put this loveseat on the level of a chaise lounge and adapt it for use next to a pool.

● **CAPTURE IT BETWEEN LARGE PLANTS IN A DENSE GARDEN.** The loveseat is just as usable in a setting where it will serve as a standalone bench. Blend it into a thoughtfully designed ornamental garden by positioning it next to a path and put planters on either side with tall or bushy growing shrubs or ornamental trees.

PORCH SWING

Nothing brings to mind the lazy days of late summer quite like a porch swing. It's really an invitation to slowly move back and forth, a cold glass of lemonade in your hand and nothing on your mind. A porch swing can be a sanctuary away from the hectic pace of everyday life, the perfect way to unplug and unwind. Of course, first you have to build it.

The structure of a pallet lends itself well to the stresses and strains of a hanging piece of furniture. The wood is also durable in the face of the summer thunderstorm that blows water onto the porch and over the swing. It also resists the occasional bit of dropped food or spilled iced tea during those slow, informal dinners on the porch.

This swing can be a great way to exploit an otherwise dead corner of the porch—just make sure you leave plenty of room for the swing's modest arc so that it doesn't hit any house walls or, even worse, windows. Always leave at least four feet in front of and behind the swing for the swing arc.

More importantly, only hang the swing from strong structural members that can bear the weight. Not only is the swing heavy itself, it becomes all the more so with two adults sitting side by side. As long as the supporting structure overhead is secure, the swing itself will easily support two healthy adults.

For that same reason, this project was hung by chains rather than more attractive rope. Heavy-duty chain is a must if you want to ensure the swing is as safe as it is alluring.

WHAT YOU'LL NEED

TOOLS:
Measuring tape • Speed square • Carpenter's pencil • Jigsaw or reciprocating saw • Power drill and bits • Circular saw or table saw • Palm sander • Paintbrush (optional) • Bar clamps

MATERIALS:
2 pallets • 5" wood screws • 6" FastenMaster HeadLok screws • (4) 3" wood screws • (6) $5/16 \times 4$" lag eye bolts • (12) $1/4 \times 4$" lag eye screws • (4) $1/4$" carbon steel quick link • $3/16$" grade 30 zinc-plated chain • 80- and 100-grit sandpaper • Paint (optional) • Seat and back cushions (optional)

TIME: 1 HOUR **DIFFICULTY:** MEDIUM

HOW YOU MAKE IT

1. Measure and mark the faces of a pallet's stringers with a speed square: for a 15°, cut 28" from one end of the pallet. The cut should be angled down toward the back. Make the cuts with a reciprocating saw, and then square off the angle cuts of the larger section (the seat).

2. Sit the cut edges of the smaller section's (the seatback) stringers on the top edges of the seat's stringers. (You may have to remove the rearmost board on the seat so that the back's stringer ends can sit flush on top of the seat's stringers.)

3. Screw the back to the seat with 5" wood screws driven from each side of the seatback's stringers, down into the seat's stringers.

4. Carefully place the swing upside down and drive 6" HeadLok screws through the bottom edges of the seat stringers up into the back stringers.

5. Hold a deconstructed stringer diagonally across the outer faces of the seat and back, as an arm. Mark angled cuts on each end of the stringer. Make the cuts with a circular saw. Use the arm as a template to mark and cut a stringer for the opposite arm.

6. Screw the arms to the seat and back with two 3" wood screws per end, driven off center. Drill starter holes for the lag eye bolts in the arm where they overlap the seat and back stringer faces. Screw in the bolts as tightly as possible.

7. Measure the on-center spacing of the porch roof joists and cut two stringer scraps to span three joists. Face-screw these braces above where you want the swing, spaced on center equal to the outside width of the swing. Use two ¼ x 4" lag screws at each joist. Drill a starter hole and screw a lag eye screw up through each brace into the center joist.

8. Use a carbon steel quick link on each side to hang 4' sections of ³⁄₁₆"-grade 30 zinc-plated chain (you may need to adjust the chain lengths; the swing should hang 17" above the floor).

9. Sit the swing on supports 17" off the floor, and tilt it to the desired final angle. Measure from each lag eye screw to the end of the chain hanging from the roof and cut chains to those lengths.

10. Sand the surface of the swing and finish as desired. Attach the support chains to the swing's lag eye screws with quick links, and join the free ends to the roof chain with quick links. Add a seat and back cushions for comfort as desired.

HANGING PORCH SWINGS

Securely hanging a porch swing is crucial to prevent personal injury or damage to your porch and home. It's always best to err on the side of overkill when it comes to supporting large amounts of weight from a home's load-bearing structure.

To guarantee the integrity of the chain support, use a screw eye with at least a four-inch shaft. You can make installing a screw eye directly into a joist easier by drilling a pilot hole a size or two smaller than the screw eye shaft. Tighten the screw eye down by sticking a large screwdriver through the eye and slowly turning it clockwise.

If you don't have a porch, you may be tempted to hang the swing from a large, old-growth tree. This is usually not advisable because there is no way to assess the internal integrity of a tree branch, and the outer end remains unsupported. If you do decide to hang the swing from a tree, the branch must be at least eight inches in diameter, live rather than dead, with no visible damage, defects, or disease. The branch should be growing upward rather than parallel to the ground. As with porch joists, you should use a chain to hang the swing, but be aware that the chain will damage the tree over time.

One of the most stable ways to secure a porch swing to a porch ceiling is with cross braces running perpendicular to the roof joists, as shown here.

CHAISE LOUNGE

WHAT YOU'LL NEED

TOOLS:
Circular saw • Measuring tape • Carpenter's pencil • Power drill and bits • 1" spade bit • Palm sander • Paint-brush (optional) • Bar clamps

MATERIALS:
3 pallets • Construction adhesive or waterproof wood glue • 2 ½" wood screws • 3" wood screws • 4" wood screws • 2" wood screws • (2) 1 ½ x 3" stainless-steel marine butt hinges • 1 x 34" metal dowel • Sandpaper • Paint or finish (optional) • Cushion (optional)

TIME: 1.5 HOURS **DIFFICULTY:** HARD

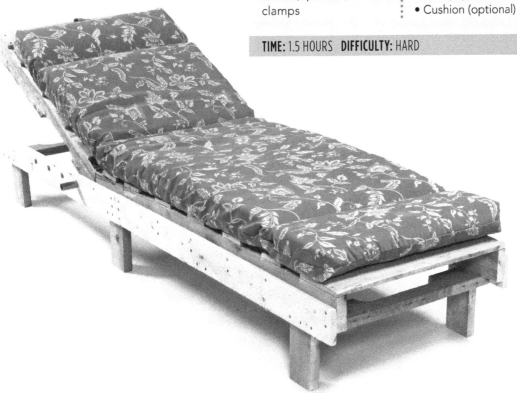

This project builds on the features that make the chaise lounge a classic piece of outdoor furniture. The length ensures that even tall people can stretch out, and the adjustable back means that the lounge is adaptable—it can be a handy put-your-legs-up place to read the morning paper and then become a nice tanning bed in the afternoon.

As with all outdoor pallet furniture, thoroughly sand all surfaces. A splintery edge can ruin any sun-drenched afternoon. No matter where you put the chaise, you'll want it looking its best. You can paint it if you prefer, but chaise lounges are traditionally finished natural or lightly stained—a waterproof finish is ideal, especially one with added UV protection. For maximum comfort, you'll also want to add a cushion.

HOW YOU MAKE IT

1. Remove the bottom deck boards from two pallets. Cut the top deck boards of both flush with one edge of the center stringer (the seat and back are both 24¾" wide, with two stringers and deck boards running flush to each side).

2. Measure and mark the stringers 46" long for the seat and 30" long for the back. Remove any deck boards that would be in the way as you make the cuts. Cut the seat and back to length. Cut two frame rails 40" long and two 36" long from deck boards (one short and one long rail will be joined to make each side frame).

3. Cut five cleats from stringers, equal to the inside width of the stringers in the pallet section you cut. Construct the double cleat by coating one face of a cleat with construction adhesive (or use waterproof wood glue) and mating a second cleat to it flush all around. Screw them together with rows of 2½" wood screws staggered every four inches.

4. Line the cleats up in a row, parallel to each other, on a flat, level, clean work surface. Lay a long and a short rail board on their faces, running together on each side of the cleats. They should be perpendicular to the cleats.

5. Position two cleats 2" in from each end of the rails. Position a third 20" from the front edge of the long rail boards. Position the double cleat bridging the butt joint between the two rail sections on each side. Mark the cleat locations on each rail board. Measure to check that the cleat marks are exactly the same on each side.

6. Flip the rail boards on one side up so that they are face to end with the cleats and so that the bottom edges of the rails are flush with the bottom faces of the cleats. Drill pilot holes and screw the rail boards to the cleats with two 3" wood screws per cleat (use four screws for the center double cleat). Repeat with the opposite side to complete the frame.

7. Cut six legs 7¾" long from stringers. Cut a 1¾" square notch in one corner of each leg (measure the cleat widths first and adjust as necessary). Attach the legs to the rails with the notches butted to the inside edges of the front and back cleats and the back edge of the double cleat. Screw the rails to the legs with 2" wood screws and the legs to the cleats by driving 4" wood screws down through the cleats and into the leg tops.

8. Notch the seat frame to sit over the top of the doubled-up frame cleat. Sit the top sections in place on the cleats, adjusting their position to line them up with the frame. Screw the rails to the seat stringers with 2" wood screws.

9. Remove deck boards as necessary to allow for placement of the hinge flanges on the cut ends of the seat and back stringers. Rip deck boards as necessary and screw them into gaps to make a fairly uniform seat and back surface. (If your stringers have notches, sister unnotched waste sections over the notches to create a flat surface flush with the

bottom of the stringer so that the back sits properly on the prop adjustment.) Screw down the hinges between seat and back stringers using 1½ × 3" stainless-steel marine butt hinges (or substitute standard 4" strap hinges by the width of your stringers).

10. With the back in the upright position, measure and mark the rails on each side for the back adjustment holes, every 4" starting 4" back from the hinge location. Drill 1" holes at the marks, 1" down from the top of the rails, using a spade bit. Slide a 1 x 34" metal rod through an adjustment hole and set the back against the dowel.

11. Sand the chaise lounge all over and finish with stain, clear finish, or paint, as desired.

QUICK 3

Certain outdoor additions add immeasurably to your yard and home but are perhaps not what you'd naturally think of fabricating. Something like the outdoor lighting fixtures opposite isn't an obvious addition to a backyard, but you're sure to wonder how you ever did without them. One of the most wonderful things about the three projects in this section is that they are easily expandable. Want to add decorative shutters to all your windows rather than just the two in your utility shed? Pick up a few more pallets and make multiples! It doesn't hurt that—like all "Quick 3" topics—these are easy and quick to build. They also lend themselves to stylizing beyond just painting. Add your own unique details and make any of these a personal design statement.

1. PLANT MARKERS

Accent a wonderful country garden with some simple plant markers that will help you and the other gardeners in your family identify exactly what was planted where. These markers are simple to craft from any pallet deck boards. Cut a board in half and rip it lengthwise in half to create the rough shapes. Cut one end of each marker to a stake point to finish the shape. Embellish the marker as you prefer, by using a jigsaw to cut a curve or other decorative flourish in the top. Hand-letter or stencil letters to create the names of plants and provide an eye-catching graphic in your yard. You can use the markers as purely informative devices, to keep track of what has been planted where, or you can leverage the look as a design feature by painting or staining the markers and using elaborate font stencils for the letters.

2. OUTDOOR LIGHTING FIXTURES

Bring a romantic touch to an outdoor sitting area or secluded corner of the yard by illuminating the space with the soft glow of votive candles in Mason jars. Cut a section of a pallet sized to meet your needs; you can use a whole pallet if you want a lot of light. Remove all but two boards on the bottom. Punch holes in the jar lids of four to six Mason jars. Screw small eye screws into the center of each lid (or devise your own hanging solution, such as wrapping the neck of each jar in stripped copper wire, screwing the lid down over the wire, and hanging the jar from the ends). Screw matching eye screws into the pallet's top deck boards for each of the Mason jars. Finish the pallet as you prefer. Screw sturdy ceiling hooks into the stringers of the pallet and hang it from a tree branch with chain or rope or attach it directly to the overhang of a pergola or an arbor. Hang the jars by wire if that's what you used to secure the jars or use small-gauge chains run between the eye screw in the jar lids and the corresponding eye screw in the pallet. In either case, unscrew the lid from each jar, set a votive candle inside, light it, and let the nighttime magic begin.

3. WINDOW SHUTTERS

Years ago, in areas of the country where fall and winter could bring brutal weather, functional window shutters were the norm. They were ways to protect the home against damage, but they were eventually adopted by builders as more of an architectural ornament than a functional piece of a building. You can build decorative shutters to spruce up a backyard shed, outbuilding, or even your house. Start by measuring half the width of the window or windows for which you want the shutters. The simplest way to construct the shutters is to cut deck boards to the measured width, and arrange them parallel to one another, in a column matching the window's height. Join the boards by running two stringers face down and side by side (but separated by a couple of inches) from the bottom to the top of the shutter. Screw the stringers to the deck boards with countersunk wood screws. Thoroughly sand the shutter all over, prime, and paint it a color that complements or contrasts the building's siding. You'll want to add shutters to both sides of a window. You can go further by drilling or cutting decorative profiles on the stringers or boards or stenciling them.

PLANTER BENCH

The planter bench is a garden furniture hybrid that continues to grow in popularity. That's because it does double duty, with each part of the structure making the other more enjoyable.

This version includes planters on both sides of the bench. The supports for the bench itself are actually built into the walls of the planters on each side. That gives the structure an appealing symmetry and makes it ideal for just about anywhere you need outdoor seating—from a deck to a patio to a shady spot along a garden pathway.

Although the finished project is a spectacular and useful piece of outdoor furniture, it does require attention to detail. Be careful with all the measurements (remember: "measure twice, cut once"), and pay

attention to the fine points of how the bench is integrated into the construction of the planters.

The bench is large enough for two people to sit side by side comfortably. The planters can accommodate many different plants and are large enough to support even small ornamental trees such as a mock orange. For a really powerful first impression, plant perfumed plants such as fragrant roses, rosemary, sage, or jasmine. You can also grow vining plants by adding a trellis. Just keep in mind that whatever you plant should not encroach upon the sitting area of the bench, or the bench won't be inviting.

The planter bench looks best left unfinished so that it weathers to a lovely gray, or finished in a light stain or clear polyurethane. Depending on where you use it, and whether you're going to add sprawling plants to the planters (which will tumble over the sides and partially hide the planters), you can use extremely rough planter wood.

WHAT YOU'LL NEED

TOOLS:
Pry bar or hammer • Power drill and bits • Circular saw or table saw • 4 F-style clamps • Palm sander • Staple gun

MATERIALS:
3 pallets • 3" finish nails • 2" wood screws • 3" wood screws • 80- and 100-grit sandpaper • Clear finish (optional) • Landscape fabric

TIME: 2 HOURS **DIFFICULTY:** HARD

HOW YOU MAKE IT

1. Deconstruct three pallets. Build the seat frame using two unnotched stringers (or two clear 2×4s if your stringers are notched) and two 14½" cleats cut from separate stringers. Create the box frame with the cleats running between the rails at either end.

2. Cut ten seat slats 17½" long from deck boards (if your deck boards are thin, you might consider using true 1×4s for added strength). Space the slats out evenly across the tops of the stringer rails. Drill pilot holes and nail the slats to the rails with two finish nails at each end of each board.

3. Cut forty 18"-long panel boards from deck boards. Build the planters' front and back panels by laying two 22" trim pieces cut from stringers (so that any notches are centered along the length of the trim pieces) parallel on a clean, level work surface. (Adjust your measurements if your stringers are not 1½" thick or your deck boards are not ¾" thick—those are the measurements on which these dimensions are based.) Lay five panel boards across the trim pieces and adjust so that the top and bottom edges are all flush and the trim overhangs the panel boards 2¼" on each side. Screw the panel boards to the trim using 2" wood screws.

4. Construct the two outside planter panels by repeating the process with 17½" trim boards and no overhang.

5. Partially construct the planters by screwing a front and back panel to an outside panel by drilling pilot holes and driving 3" wood screws through the top and bottom trim pieces where they overlap.

6. Attach the inside panel bottom trim to the partially constructed boxes with the panels upright. Use four F-style clamps to hold the bench in position as you drill pilot holes and screw the top front and back panel trim to the side of the seat rails with 3" wood screws. The top of the seat should be flush with the top of the boxes. Repeat with the opposite side.

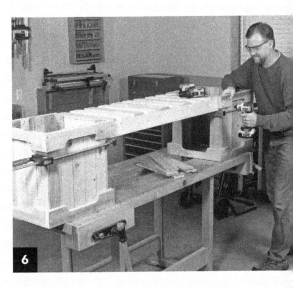

7. Use 2" wood screws to attach the five panel boards vertically to the bench end and inside panel bottom trim. Repeat for the opposite planter.

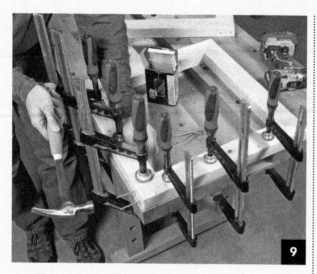

9. Clamp the caps together on a work surface, and drill pilot holes through the miters (if your deck boards are thin, pocket screw the joints together). Nail the miter joints together with finish nails to construct the cap frames. Center the cap frames on the top of each planter, drill pilot holes, and nail the caps down to the trim.

10. Sand the bench and planter thoroughly. Stain, paint, or finish the structure with a clear finish. Line the inside of each planter with landscape fabric folded and stapled so that it is flush to the panels. Fill the planters with dirt and plant shrubs, miniature trees, or your favorite flowering perennials.

8. Cut four back and front panel caps 22" long from deck boards (adjust as necessary if your stringers and deck boards are thinner than 1½" and ¾"). Cut four side-panel caps 20 ½" long (we used 2×4s here). Cut 45° miters in all cap ends.

PLANTER BENCH STRATEGIES

There are many ways to build on or optimize the basic idea of this planter bench. Here are a few, but you're sure to come up with some on your own.

● **EXTEND, EXTEND, EXTEND.** The technique used in this project to integrate the bench in the inner wall of each planter can be replicated to add a bench on the opposite sides of the planters—making a long run of seating ideal for bordering a wall or fence in a long, narrow garden. You can also integrate a bench into the perpendicular planter wall to make a pair of benches and three planters to go into the corner of a patio or deck.

● **ADD A CUSHION.** Although the look of the bench is most traditional when left bare, a cushion would make the bench more comfortable for extended periods of sitting. This is especially useful if an elderly or infirm person will be tending the planters on each side.

● **PLAN FOR WATER.** When you're picking out the location of your planter bench unit, it's wise to think about how you'll be watering the plants. Ideally, situate the unit near a garden bed from which you can extend drip irrigation into the planters. That way, the plants in the planters will require little or no maintenance, making this an even more enjoyable garden structure.

ADIRONDACK CHAIR

The iconic design of this chair can trace its roots back a century, but the look—and, more importantly, the comfort—of this classic chair is timeless. It features an alluring combination of a perfectly slanted back with wide arms that invite relaxation. Even without a cushion, the chair is remarkably comfortable. You can spend hours in one without ever becoming stiff.

The version in this project is fairly easy to construct thanks to some crafting shortcuts. The design is also forgiving of slight mistakes. With a couple of cuts, you can easily change the angle of the recline and the angle of the legs, if they are not to your liking.

The look of the finished chair fits right in with other outdoor furniture, complementing Chaise Lounges (see page 37), more conventional patio chairs, and even brick benches. The chair is also lightweight enough to be relatively portable. Use it on the deck for casual conversations over a drink with friends, and then move it to the far reaches of the yard for a private weekend reading session.

Don't worry about jostling it as you move it around—the construction is durable and resilient, even in the face of spills, weather, and the occasional sprinkler soaking.

WHAT YOU'LL NEED

TOOLS:
Circular saw or table saw • Power drill and bits • Measuring tape • Carpenter's pencil • Jigsaw • Carpenter's square • Level • Palm sander • Paintbrush

MATERIALS:
2 pallets • 2" wood screws • 1 ½ " wood screws • 3" wood screws • Trammel compass • Finish nails • Wood putty • 80- and 100-grit sandpaper • Paint

TIME: 1 HOUR **DIFFICULTY:** MEDIUM

HOW YOU MAKE IT

1. Cut six seatback boards 35" long from deck boards. Orient them vertically and place them in a row on a flat, level work surface. Use spacers to maintain a ½" gap between each board.

2. Cut a lower cross brace 23½" long from a stringer. Screw it across the bottom of the seatback boards, flush with the sides and bottoms, using 2" wood screws.

3. Measure and mark the horizontal center line of the seatback. Cut a 19½"-long upper cross brace from a deck board. Center it side to side, with the bottom edge aligned on the center line. Screw it to the seatback boards with 1½" wood screws.

4. On the front of the seatback, measure and mark points 10" down from the two middle seatback boards, with the points centered side to side. Drive a nail at each point. Use these points for a trammel compass, set at 10". Scribe semicircles from the top of each board, off to the side.

5. Use a jigsaw to cut the boards along the arc cut line.

6. Cut two 33" legs from unnotched stringers (or 2×4s if your stringers are notched). Cut a fascia board and five seat slats 26½" long from deck boards. Screw the fascia across the ends of the legs with 2" wood screws.

7. Line the seat slats up along the legs starting at the fascia board. Maintain a ½" gap between each board. Drill pilot holes and fasten the slats to the legs with finish nails.

8. Fasten the back to the seat legs by sliding the back down between the legs perpendicular to the seat. The top of the seatback's lower brace should be even with the top edge of the legs. Screw the legs to the seatback's lower cross brace with three 3" wood screws on each side.

9. Cut the front legs 20" long from a stringer. Measure and mark a line 15" up from what will be the bottom of each leg. Line these reference lines up with the top of the seat on each side. Tack the legs

in place and check with a carpenter's square to ensure they are perfectly perpendicular to the seat. Screw them to the long legs with 3" wood screws.

10. Sit the chair on a flat, level work surface. Use a level to mark a cut line across the bottom of the front and back legs, and a matching line across the top of the front legs. Make the cuts with a circular saw.

11. Cut two wide deck boards 30" long for the arms. Measure and mark 3" in from the side along one end. Mark a line from the mark to the diagonal corner at the other end. Cut the tapers on both arms.

12. Hold the arms on both sides level between the top of the front legs and the sides of the seatback (use a level to check placement). Mark the sides of the seatback for the arm brace position. Cut the arm brace 29 ½" long from a stringer. Screw it to the back of the seatback, with the top edge aligned with the marks, using 2" wood screws.

13. Screw the arms to the braces and front legs, using 2" wood screws. Putty over the screwheads. Sand the chair all over.

JIGSAW MAGIC

A jigsaw is an especially useful tool when it comes to custom fabricating a project like the **Adirondack Chair** out of pallet wood. It can make cutting curves, arcs, and even complex shapes almost as simple as marking the shape. Of course, a jigsaw is ideal in other situations as well. You can use it to make simple, quick crosscuts of thinner members such as deck boards. That means a jigsaw can be a great way of trimming all the deck boards in a pallet along one edge of the center stringer when you're cutting the pallet down to make a project two stringers wide. The tool is also the classic solution for finishing the inside corners of intersecting circular saw cuts, to prevent overcutting.

Regardless of what you'll be cutting with the jigsaw, here are a few guidelines to use it to its best advantage.

● **CUT SLOWLY.** This is a good idea not only to accurately follow a curving or complex cut line, but also to keep the blade from bending during any cut, which can lead to beveled cut edges rather than sharp, crisp cut surfaces.

● **KEEP THE SHOE FLAT ON THE BOARD.** This will help you accurately follow a cut line. Remember to cut on the outside of the cut line and sand back as necessary.

● **USE A FINER BLADE.** Pallet wood is already rough by nature, so it's best not to make coarse cuts and add to your sanding burden. A blade with at least ten teeth per inch is ideal. You can also help prevent chipping by taping the cut area with painter's tape and drawing the cut line on top of the tape.

BUYING THE RIGHT JIGSAW

If you're going to make your pallet projects as easy as possible to execute, it's wise to buy a jigsaw that will do everything you need it to do. Look for a model with a one-quarter-inch universal tang that holds the blade in place with a set screw. This will allow you to buy any brand of blade. If you plan on using the jigsaw often, you may want to look for one with orbital cutting action, which will position the blade at a more aggressive angle to cut through wood more easily. Opting for a longer blade stroke, such as 1", will also reduce the amount of time it takes to get through a cut. Any saw equipped with blade guides will cut more accurately and with less bending and binding. Lastly, choose a saw with variable speeds, an incredibly

handy feature. It's especially useful if you're going to be making some of the tricky cuts in more adventurous pallet projects.

CENTRAL AC UNIT SCREEN

WHAT YOU'LL NEED

TOOLS:
Reciprocal saw or frameless hacksaw • Cutting pliers • Nippers • Circular saw • Power drill and bits • Miter saw • Palm sander • Paintbrush (optional)

MATERIALS:
3 pallets • 2" deck screws • 3" deck screws • Sandpaper, 80 grit • Paint or stain (optional)

TIME: 1 HOUR   **DIFFICULTY:** MEDIUM

Your home exhibits your sense of style. It's why you work so hard on keeping your yard in tip-top shape, and why any homeowner goes to the trouble of picking out paint and the hard work of putting it on the house. It's all about curb appeal. Aside from the pride you feel when your house looks great, it's also a way to maintain a big part of the value of the structure.

Unfortunately, many of a home's fixtures and exterior features—like exposed power meters and hose bibs—work to the detriment of curb appeal. The savvy homeowner puts in a little extra effort to conceal those blemishes. That's where this screen comes in.

One of the biggest visual offenders—especially on upscale homes—is the main AC condenser unit placed alongside the house on its own concrete pad. Not only are these units big visuals, but they are also just plain ugly. Disguising that ugliness is a great use for a few pallets and half an afternoon's worth of effort.

In fact, done right, you'll turn an eyesore area into a showstopping feature. It's all about getting creative with what is a very basic design. You can drill patterns into the deck boards of this screen, paint the final structure in an innovative or incredibly sophisticated color scheme, or ornament the wood with decorative metal accents. The possibilities are just a matter of engaging your imagination. The only caveat is to be sure that you maintain good air circulation around the AC unit so that it can perform its all-important function.

HOW YOU MAKE IT

1. Carefully remove the two outer stringers of one pallet by cutting the fasteners with a reciprocating saw or frameless hacksaw. Remove or clip off any remaining fasteners sticking out from the underside of the deck board ends.

2. Clean up the removed stringers, pulling out or grinding down any protruding fasteners. Remove all the end bottom boards on two different pallets.

3. Drill pilot holes centered on each end of each deck board on the pallet for which you removed the two side stringers. Working on a flat, level surface, stand this pallet up perpendicular to one of the prepared pallets. Screw each deck board to the end stringer of the perpendicular pallet with 2" deck screws.

4. Miter one end of the deck boards you removed to 45°. Miter both ends of a third board to 45°.

5. Position the top frame pieces on top of the screen, with the mitered joints at the front and the notches, if any, facing the AC unit. Screw the frame pieces to the stringer ends on both sides and in front, using 3" deck screws.

Optional: Use the leftover deck boards to create an ornamental top to the screen. Cut each end of each board in half circles or to points and position them on the top frame running side to side, with equal spacing front to back. Drill pilot holes and screw them down to the top frame.

6. Sand the screen all over as necessary to make it look more presentable, and then coat with the finish of your choice. (Choose a stain or paint to blend the screen with the siding of the house.)

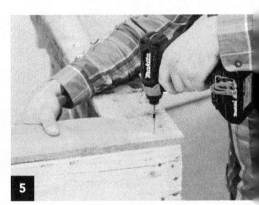

POTTING BENCH

Every gardener knows that you need a center of operations, a staging area where you can work on an elevated surface rather than bending over or kneeling on the ground. It has to be rugged and easy to clean, and there should be plenty of room for gardening tasks small and large. That, in a nutshell, is why gardeners in the know never tackle their yard or garden beds without a trusty potting bench tucked into a large shed or a corner of the backyard.

Of course, there are potting benches and then there are potting benches. This one checks all the right boxes. Crafted of durable pallet wood, it is impervious to the dynamic duo of gardening: water and dirt. Cleanup entails nothing more than brushing dirt and debris off the top surface or, occasionally, hosing the thing down.

You can use it to store tools and supplies as well. A roomy bottom shelf is the perfect location for a bag or two of potting soil or composted manure. The hooks on the side mean that you can hang garden tools such as a trowel right where you need them and use them most. Use the opposite side for extra hoses or extension cords.

Although this is a sizable project, it's not highly technical. It takes a bit of time, but the expense will be pleasantly minimal. The most crucial part of the building process is measuring and cutting accurately. Take your time and check your measurements often, because accuracy is crucial to ensuring the bench stands stable and strong. But make it right, and this structure could easily last a decade or more, even under hard use.

HOW YOU MAKE IT

1. Fabricate the legs from two pallets. Remove all the deck boards from the bottom of each pallet with a frameless hacksaw. Cut the deck boards on the other side of both pallets along one edge of the center stringer. Measure and mark the stringers 35¼" from one end, ideally along the edge of one deck board, and cut with a circular saw. *Note: The cut end will be the top of the legs on each side and the measurement can vary by 1" one way or another to allow a deck board to run along the top edge of each leg pair. However, if a deck board is in the way of the cut, remove it.*

2. Remove all but the two deck boards closest to the cut end on each leg pair. Clip the opposite end of each stringer to create feet. Measure and mark 5" up each stringer edge opposite the deck boards, measuring from the uncut end. Measure and mark the center of the uncut end. Use a straightedge to connect the marks, and then cut along this line on each of the stringers.

3. Carefully measure and mark a third pallet for the top and bottom shelves and back of the bench. Mark the stringer cuts for one shelf 17¾" from the ends of the stringers. Mark for the second shelf 17¾" up from those marks, and for the back, 12" up from those marks. Make the cuts on each stringer, removing deck boards as necessary.

4. Prep the top shelf by removing any deck boards within 3½" of either end.

5. Precisely align the top edge of the top shelf side stringer (the top is the side with the deck boards) and the unclipped end of the leg stringers, and then screw the leg stringers to the ends of the top shelf stringer with 3" deck screws. Repeat the process with the second leg pair on the opposite side of the top shelf.

3

6. Measure and mark 12" up from the bottom of each leg. Align the top edge of one bottom shelf side stringer with the marks on one leg pair and check for square with a speed square. Screw the legs to the ends of the bottom shelf side stringers with 3" deck screws. Repeat the process on the opposite leg pair and the opposite side of the bottom deck.

7. Cut two 2x4s to 40" (or use waste stringers if possible). Screw each to one end of the back's stringers to create a box frame for the back. Stand the back in position, with the back edges of the stringers aligned with the back face of the leg pairs. Screw the back to the top shelf stringers.

8. Position an uncut deck board across the top, aligned with the front face of the leg stringers. Drill pilot holes and screw the board to the top's stringers with 3" deck screws.

6 **7**

Optional: Screw uncut deck boards across the underside of the top shelf to create storage pockets. Rip deck boards as needed to fill in overlarge gaps. Although the top is meant to allow soil and water to pass through easily, you can create a solid work surface over all or part of the top by cutting a top from ¼" exterior-grade plywood and screwing it down.

9. Screw hanging hooks in convenient locations on the leg pair deck boards and the inside face of the back as desired. If the table wobbles on a flat, level surface, either trim the leg pair stringers as necessary or use adjustable screw feet on the bottom of the legs.

STRAWBERRY BOX

threat to your strawberry harvest. Gardeners fight the onslaught by planting their strawberries in protected, controlled containers—such as a box like this.

It should be obvious that you have to be careful about the type of pallet you choose for the box. Any that has been used to transport chemicals should not be used for this project; the soil, plants, fruit, and the water they drink will all come into significant contact with the wood.

The beautiful strawberry is the jewel of the summer garden. Luscious, sweet, and eye-catching, strawberries are a welcome addition to a summer harvest.

For all their wonderful attributes, though, strawberries can be a little challenging to grow. They need lots of sun and nutritious, well-drained soil. And though each individual plant is small, they like to have a lot of room around them to spread out through what's known as runners and stolons (which can become new plants). They are also the target of several garden pests that enjoy the sweet treat every bit as much as humans do. Garden slugs, in particular, are a constant

The project construction is fairly simple. The biggest challenge you will face is removing some deck boards and possibly repositioning them. A good frameless hacksaw—or better yet, reciprocating saw—will make that process easy. Beyond the steps outlined here, you probably don't need to change anything or dress the box up. As dirty and exposed to the elements as it will be, it doesn't make sense to paint or stain the box. However, you can add casters to the feet to make the box portable so that it can be rolled into a greenhouse or shed off season.

WHAT YOU'LL NEED

TOOLS:
Frameless hacksaw or reciprocating saw • Circular saw • Measuring tape • Marker • Bar clamps • Power drill and bits • Staple gun and staples • Kreg pocket hole jig

MATERIALS:
Pallet • 3" deck screws • Scrap 2x4 • Landscape fabric • Topsoil or potting soil • Strawberry plants • 2 ½" pocket hole screws

CUT LIST:
(8) ¾ x 3 ½ x 15" end slats • (8) ¾ x 3 ½ x 38 ½" side slats • (6) 1 ½ x 3 ½ x 15" frame stiles • (6) 1 ½ x 3 ½ x 8" frame rails • (4) ¾ x 3 ½ x 40" floor-boards • (4) 1 ½ x 3 ½ x 5" feet

TIME: 45 MINUTES **DIFFICULTY:** EASY

HOW YOU MAKE IT

1. Deconstruct two pallets. Cut all pieces from stringers and the deck boards to the measurements on the cut list.

2. Use a pocket hole jig to drill two pocket holes in each end of each frame rail. Lay out a frame with the two rails between the inside edges of two stiles so that outside edges are flush all around. Check square by measuring diagonals (they should match) and then screw the rails to the stiles with 2 ½" pocket hole screws.

3. Repeat the process to build the remaining two frames. Clamp them in place to a work surface with the end frames 40" apart and the center frame centered between the two. Drill pilot holes and screw four side slats spaced equidistant top to bottom, with their ends flush with the outer edges of the frames. Repeat on the opposite side.

4. Drill pilot holes and screw end slats with each end overlapping the ends of the side slats, top to bottom on one end. Repeat on the opposite end.

5. Drill pilot holes and screw the floorboards spaced evenly across the bottoms of the frames.

6. Staple landscape fabric around the inside of the box. Position the box in an area that gets at least six hours of direct sun a day. Ideally, the box should be positioned so that both sides get an equal amount of sun. If one side is shaded, you may want to leave that side unplanted.

7. Add topsoil or potting soil up to the first gap in the side boards. Cut the fabric and push strawberry plants into the soil through the cuts.

Optional: To accommodate large starts, you may want to drill through the side slats with a 1" spade bit. Plants should be 18" apart. Add plants at the ends in the same way. Once you've reached the top, plant several strawberry plants around the top surface with the same spacing, and then water thoroughly. Cover the soil around the plants with sawdust to discourage snails and slugs.

WORKBENCH

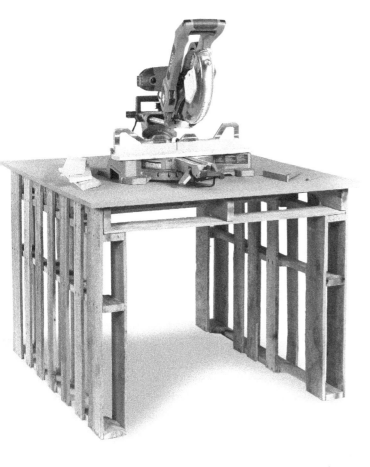

Who doesn't need a sturdy workbench?

Indoors or out, a workbench is an incredibly handy structure, as a place to park tools and supplies and a rugged surface for crafting projects small and large. When it comes to simple, durable, tough, and portable workbenches, you'll be hard-pressed to top the one in this project.

It's basically just three pallets combined in a way that ensures a durable work surface, one on which you won't be afraid to chop, drill, cut, or splash paint.

Leave it out in the yard during a rainstorm? No worries. It's pallet wood after all. It will take all that the elements can throw at it and be ready for you when you start your next project.

It's also a compact, portable table. All you need is a helper to move it anywhere you want to work. Once you get it there, you'll find that the workbench supports a surprising amount of weight. Pile a chop saw, portable grinder, or other power tool right on top without worrying about the table getting wobbly.

HOW YOU MAKE IT

1. Modify two pallets for the workbench legs. Cut the top deck boards 35 ¼" long. Cut the bottom deck boards 31" long (or the length of the top deck boards minus the thickness of the pallets you're using, including top and bottom deck boards—the pallets used here were 4 ¼" thick).

2. Remove the board remnants from both sides of the stringer that was removed from each leg when you made the board cuts. Screw it in place between the legs' top and bottom deck boards, with the top face flush with the top of the shorter boards on the legs.

3. Stand the legs in place, parallel to each other and with the cut sides up (you can brace them by tacking a waste deck board edge to edge across the legs).

4. Nest the edges of a full pallet, bottom side down, into the cutouts at the top of the two legs.

5. Use a carpenter's square to check that the legs are plumb to the top. Screw the legs' outside deck boards to the top's stringers on both sides, using 3" wood screws.

6. Drive 4" wood screws up through the legs' top stringers into the top surface's stringers on both sides.

7. Add a top working surface to the workbench, such as a sheet of ¾" plywood (used here) or medium-density fiberboard. Nail it down with brads. You can cut it to match the dimensions of the table exactly, or allow for 2 to 3" of overhang, as with this table.

TOSS ACROSS GAME BOARDS

WHAT YOU'LL NEED

TOOLS:
Frameless hacksaw or reciprocating saw • Circular saw • Compass or trammel • Measuring tape • Carpenter's pencil • Clamps • Jigsaw • Framing square • Power drill and bits • Palm sander • Paintbrush (optional) • Hammer

MATERIALS:
2 pallets • 3" deck screws • (4) 2 x 4 x 12" legs • (4) ½ x 4" carriage bolts • (4) ½" washers • (4) ½" nuts • 80-grit sandpaper • 1" brads • Exterior paint

TIME: 40 MINUTES **DIFFICULTY:** EASY

No backyard entertaining setup can be considered complete without this endlessly fun game, also known as cornhole. It is a classic of lazy summer weekend get-togethers and requires nothing more than the boards made with this project, a few beanbags, and some friends you can play with.

Although crafted from modified pallets, these boards are actually incredibly close to the regulation toss across board dimensions (forty-eight by twenty-four inches with a six-inch-diameter hole). Buy some three-and-a-half-inch beanbags—four in one color and four in another—and you're good to go.

Once you've completed the boards, they are set up twenty-seven feet apart, front edge to front edge (the hole is at the back). A team can be one or two people playing against a team of the same size. The object is to score points by throwing the beanbags into the hole or by landing them on the top of the board. The teams alternate throwing, and a player's foot

cannot go past the front of their own board, or that throw doesn't count. Scoring is simple for kids and adults alike: any bag that lands and sits on the board's surface equals one point. A bag thrown through the hole nets you three points. Misses are zero.

Once each side has thrown their beanbags, the round is finished and the points are added up. Whichever team scores higher, the other team's score is subtracted from that score. The points remaining are the points earned. The first team to snag twenty-one points takes home the big prize (whatever that may be). A toss across match is the best of three games. The winning team must always win by at least two points, or play continues until one team moves two points ahead.

Fun and simple competition, the game never seems to grow old—especially with the sun to your back and a cold beverage in your free hand!

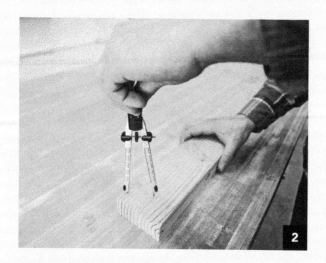

HOW YOU MAKE IT

1. With a frameless hacksaw, remove the deck boards from the bottom of a pallet. Cut the top deck boards along the edge of the center stringer. Repeat the process with a second pallet.

2. Remove the deck board fragments from one of the waste stringers and use a circular saw to cut the stringer into four 12" legs. Set the two points of a compass or trammel 1³/₄" apart. Measure down 1³/₄" from one end of each leg and make a mark that is centered side to side. Use this mark to position the point of the trammel or compass and draw an arc, with a 1³/₄" radius, across the end of the leg.

3. Clamp the leg securely to a work surface and use the jigsaw to cut the arc in the end of the leg. Use the first leg as a template to mark the three remaining legs and cut the arcs as you did with the first leg.

4. Measure and mark the hole in the first board. Use a framing square to measure and mark the center of the hole exactly 9" from the end and 12" in from one side. (Depending on the location of the deck boards, one end will probably work better.)

5. Rip a deck board to fill in any gap that will interrupt the hole and screw it to the stringers after drilling pilot holes. Use a compass or trammel to mark a 6" circle around the center point.

6. Cut deck boards 24" long for the game's face boards. You'll need 14 boards per frame if your deck boards are uniform. However, it's likely you'll have to compensate for variations. Rip the deck boards as necessary to butt them together and create a solid surface on the frames. Dry fit all of them prior to screwing down to be sure the top will be square with the frame.

7. Drill pilot holes in the end of each deck board, down into the frame, and screw the boards to the frame with 3" deck screws.

8. Flip the frames over. Cut four deck boards 44" long. Position one running top to bottom on the underside of the 24" deck boards, 2" in from the inner edges of the frame sides. Tack these support boards in place with 1" brads.

9. Flip the frames right side up, drill pilot holes in each deck board, and screw the deck boards to the support boards with 1" wood screws.

10. Use a framing square to measure and mark the center of the hole for the first game board exactly 9" from the end, and 12" in from one side. Use a compass or trammel to mark a 6" circle around the center point.

11. Use a ½" bit to drill a starter hole right inside the line of the marked circle. Start a jigsaw in this hole and carefully cut out the circle. Repeat the hole measuring, marking, and cutting process on the second board.

8

12. Set one of the boards on a work table, standing it up with a long side facing down. Lay a leg on this side piece inside the frame and line up the edges. Now position the end of the leg with the arch so it's 1" away from the inside corner of the frame.

13. Use a ½" bit to drill a hole at the center mark you used to draw the arc on the leg. Drill all the way down through the frame (with a sacrificial piece underneath the frame side or holding that portion of the frame off the work surface). Repeat the process with a second leg on the opposite frame side, and then with the two remaining legs and the second frame.

11

14. Attach the legs to both frames with carriage bolts, washers, and nuts holding each leg. Use a palm sander to sand the Toss-Across boards all over. Prime and paint them your preferred color scheme (normally contrasting colors) with exterior paint.

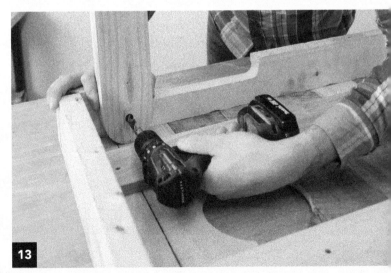

13

QUICK 3

One of the great features of pallets is that they can be stacked, butted together, and arranged like rough-hewn building blocks in an incredible diversity of configurations. The three projects here are simple garden structures that require little in the way of engineering, expertise, or exacting precision. They're crude, but useful. They're also exceptionally adaptable. You can cut down the Vertical Planter, for instance, to fit the available space on a wall or fence. No matter how you play with the designs of these, the basic function of each structure doesn't vary. Neither does the fact that they are all extremely practical. A vertical planter allows you to grow a kitchen herb garden in a limited amount of space—or create a cascading living wall with sprawling foliage plants. Pathway pavers can create a garden path wherever you need one with maximum flexibility and a minimum of fuss. And a compost bin doesn't need to be pretty or complicated to produce "black gold" for your soil and your garden plants. There's no denying that these three are not inherently the most beautiful things you'll make with pallets. That's not the point. The real sell is their utility and the fact that each of these only takes a few minutes of your time and some basic tools to put together. And yet, they're sure to last as long—or longer—than any store-bought alternatives.

1. PATHWAY PAVERS

There are so many creative possibilities opened up by simply deconstructing a pallet, but this is one of the best uses to which you can put that wood. It leverages the naturally durable nature of the wood—resistant as it is to abuse and even weather. Create an eye-catching pathway to and from a pool or just meandering through the garden, with nothing more than the leftovers from a couple of pallets used in other projects. Mark and dig out the path you want to follow (straight lines are always easiest). Dig channels for the stringers to lay on edge. Then either embed cut deck boards (twenty inches is a good path size) into a foundation of sand or screw side to side across the top of the edge stringers.

2. COMPOST BIN

A compost bin is a must-have for a productive garden and an environmentally responsible household. The structure lets you turn much of your kitchen waste into gardening black gold. Simply set three pallets on edge with the stringer faces lying on the ground, and screw the pallets together at the corners to create a U shape. Place the bin in a discreet corner of the garden and add kitchen and yard waste on a regular basis. Water your compost pile regularly, but don't allow it to become soaked. Never put animal waste, fats, meats or other proteins, or baked goods into the pile. Turn the compost at least once a week, and in a couple of months, you'll have a wonderful soil amendment.

3. HANDY VERTICAL PLANTER

Garden space limited? Don't worry—garden up rather than out by planting your own customized vertical planter. You'll use the top deck boards for mounting the planter to the surface where it will receive the most light. The planter couldn't be easier to construct. Remove bottom deck boards from a pallet, leaving only the ends and middle boards. Fold landscape fabric into pockets to fit the cavities behind the remaining boards, and dry fit them. Once you're happy with the fit, use a staple gun to staple the fabric pockets into place. Mount the planter on a wood fence or wood siding with screws, or attach it to a cyclone fence by drilling holes through the boards and wiring the planter to the fence. In either case, use more fasteners than you think necessary, because the weight of wet soil and mature plants can easily more than double the dry weight of the planter. If you're looking for an easier solution, just lean the pallet planter up against a vertical surface; it isn't likely to budge once you have planted it. The more important consideration is that the sun exposure in the location you've chosen is adequate for the plants you've selected. Ideally,

you'll want six to eight hours of direct sun for most edible plants; shade-loving plants will tolerate considerably less sun. Plant the planter with your favorite herbs, shallow-rooted vegetables, or bushy flowers, but keep in mind the mature spacing. Because the plants are growing in the best possible soil, with optimal watering, they'll definitely fill out to larger than their normal mature sizes.

POOL NOODLE AND TOWEL RACK

WHAT YOU'LL NEED

TOOLS:
Frameless hacksaw or reciprocating saw • Measuring tape • Carpenter's pencil • Circular saw • Power drill and bits • Palm sander • Paintbrush

MATERIALS:
1 pallet • ¾ x 7½ x 20" pine shelf • 2" stainless steel wood screws • 80-grit sandpaper • Primer • Exterior paints • ¾ x 24" wood dowel (curtain rod) • 2 ceiling mount curtain rod holders • 3" deck screws

TIME: 30 MINUTES **DIFFICULTY:** MEDIUM

Maybe this isn't an essential addition to every home on the block, but if you're fortunate enough to own a pool, this project is going to be an organizational boon.

Using the pallet's natural structure, with openings at either end, this rack stores a wealth of pool noodles, other flotation devices, other odds and ends, and towels and bathing suits. It can be an all-in-one tidy-up solution for your pool area, especially if you have a gang of kids regularly congregating around your outdoor water feature.

The structure includes both hanging hooks and a towel bar (towels dry more quickly and completely on a bar) to accommodate different needs and items. The hooks are perfect for bathing suits that have to dry between swim sessions, or even the odds and ends like swim caps or goggles. The shelf adds useful storage. Use it to keep small items like pool toys or other necessary items in one convenient location.

The rack is incredibly simple to build and easy to modify to your own needs. Eliminate the shelf and add hooks if hanging storage is your big requirement. You can build more than one for a large pool that is used by a lot of people or change the design in other ways—the structure is extremely adaptable.

However, because this is such a prominent feature poolside, the paint scheme is more important than with any other project in the book. A tropical, two-color scheme is a no-brainer, but you can paint it one color to make things easier on yourself, or choose a totally unique color scheme to really make the rack a design feature. No matter what it looks like, it will still be super useful!

HOW YOU MAKE IT

1. With a frameless hacksaw, remove all but the deck boards at either end from the bottom of the pallet. Cut the second and third deck boards in from one end of the top. Cut along one edge of the center stringer and along the inside edge of the outside stringer on that side.

2. Measure the pine shelf to fit in the open space along the cut edges of the boards on the center stringer (this space will be unique to whichever pallet you're using) and cut with a circular saw. Screw the shelf onto the stringer with 2" stainless steel wood screws.

3. Sand, prime, and paint the dowel that will be used as a towel bar, including the ends. Lightly sand the pallet and shelf all over, prime, and paint with the contrasting tropical colors, or in the color scheme you prefer.

4. Measure and mark 24" in from the end along the outside of the outside stringer opposite the shelf gap. Screw one ceiling mount bracket into the face of the stringer at the end and one at the 24" mark. Slide the painted dowel through the bracket openings and lock it in place with the bracket set screws.

5. Screw stainless steel hooks to the deck boards next to the shelf gap 2" down from what will be the top of the rack, and a second set of hooks 4" up from the bottom of those same deck boards.

6. Mount the rack on a fence or a wall by screwing one or more of the stringers to the fence's top rail, or by screwing the bottom two deck boards directly to the fence or wall surface.

CHAPTER THREE

STOW IN STYLE

The right storage in the right place is key to fully enjoying your home. Tripping over toys, or having to move jackets just to sit down in your own living room, is the opposite of fun and a catalyst for frustration.

That's what makes this chapter so very important, and why the projects here are sure to resonate with you. That's especially true if you have kids or are managing a large family. The more people who live in a space, the more chaotic and cluttered it becomes—and the more essential proper storage features are.

The projects here serve your storage needs both inside and outside the home. Whether it's taming a tumble of garden tools or getting your teenager's sneaker collection under control, you'll find a solution in the pages that follow. Keep in mind that these are specifically designed for adaptability. Everyone has their own storage needs, and you can customize any project in this chapter to suit exactly what you own and the space you need to organize.

For any storage structure meant to be used inside, it's also wise to consider how it will look once installed. Although most of these are simply painted, if finished at all, you should take the opportunity to decorate the project to suit whatever room it's complementing.

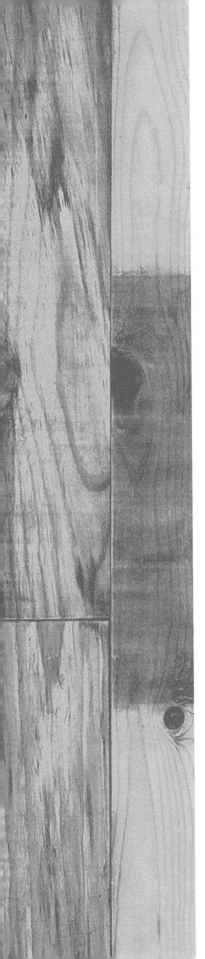
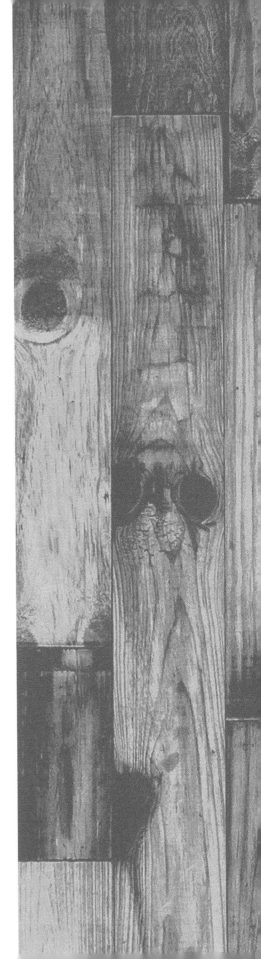

COAT RACK AND SHELF

up on the wall before the rest of the family gets home from the soccer or baseball game.

This particular rack's design is adaptable. You can resize the rack to suit your available wall space or to add decorative elements that match your home's look. The finish you choose and the hooks you include will both set the tone of the rack and determine whether it becomes an entryway focal point or blends almost invisibly with the room. You can choose from antique options that are decorative flourishes or clean chrome hooks for a more contemporary look.

The more important decision you'll have to make is the number of hooks. Make sure that you have more hooks than you need. If a coat doesn't have a place to go, it inevitably winds up draped over the back of a chair or, worse, lying on the floor somewhere. That not only makes for a clutter eyesore, it also shortens the life span of foul-weather gear.

There's just no denying that a wall-mounted coat rack can be exceptionally handy, but it's also one of those small additions to the home that homeowners never seem to get around to buying.

Why spend the money? A coat rack, like the one shown here, is an easy thing to build. You won't even need a full pallet, and you most likely have all the tools you'll need to put yours together. Start on Saturday morning and chances are you'll have it finished and

WHAT YOU'LL NEED

TOOLS:

Pry bar • Circular saw • Speed square • Power drill and bits • Pocket hole jig • Orbital sander • Stud finder • Paintbrush (optional)

MATERIALS:

1 pallet • 3" wood screws • 2 ½ " pocket hole screws • 100-grit sandpaper • Coat hooks and mounting screws • 1 quart gloss white paint (optional)

TIME: 45 MINUTES **DIFFICULTY:** EASY

HOW YOU MAKE IT

1. Remove the bottom deck boards from a pallet, and cut the stringers 16 ½" from one end, or so that there are three top deck boards remaining attached to the stringer section.

2. Use a speed square to mark the cut end of the stringers for a 45° cut. Cut the miters with a circular saw.

3. Use 3" wood screws to fasten a deck board across the uncut ends of the stringers.

4. Cut two shelves 21 ¾" long from a deck board. Use a pocket hole jig to drill pocket holes in each end. Position the shelves 3 ½" up from the bottom of the miters, and screw them in place with 2 ½" pocket hole screws.

5. Sand the unit all over and paint as desired. Screw two coat hooks onto the bottom deck board on each side of the central stringer.

6. Use a stud finder to locate the wall studs and screw the rack to the wall at the desired location with 3" wood screws. Putty over the screws, sand, and touch up the paint as necessary.

THE COAT RACK RULES

For such a simple thing, placing a coat rack thoughtfully makes all the difference between whether it is convenient and intuitive to use or a bother.

● **HEIGHT.** The Americans with Disabilities Act calls for an accessible coat rack to be placed no more than forty-eight inches from the floor. This is also an excellent rule of thumb for a house with children in it. If kids can't reach the coat rack, chances are their coats are going to wind up on a chair or on the floor. Of course, you need to accommodate all the occupants of the house, so it may make the most sense to include two coat racks—one high and one low.

● **SUPPORT.** The coat rack is screwed into studs, which is an ideal practice. If you use anchors because your coat rack placement doesn't fall neatly on studs, make sure the anchors are rated for the appropriate weight. It isn't just a matter of how much the coat rack weighs; you have to take into account the rack plus the weight of outer gear that may be wet.

● **COAT RACK PARTNERS.** Because outer gear can often be both wet and dirty, it's always wise to include some sort of absorbent mat under a coat rack. There are many types to choose from, including the informal handsome appearance of a coir mat or a miniature throw rug. The boot mats, though, are washable and dry quickly. Along with the mat, a small bench or place to sit is a natural companion—after taking off their coats, visitors or family members will probably need to take off boots or shoes to avoid tracking mud or water into the house. That is why most entryway benches are coupled with a shoe rack of one sort or another.

● **COMPATIBLE STORAGE.** A small, shallow basket for gloves, keys, or cell phones or a larger wooden bin for foul-weather footwear are both optimal complements to a coat rack—especially one like the rack in this project, featuring an integral shelf. The key to beating entryway clutter is to ensure there is a place for anything that comes in through the door.

GARDEN TOOL ORGANIZER

WHAT YOU'LL NEED

TOOLS:
Frameless hacksaw or reciprocating saw
• Circular saw • Measuring tape • Carpenter's pencil
• Power drill and bits
• 2" Forstner bit • Jigsaw
• Bar clamps

MATERIALS:
(3) 2 x 5" PVC pipe sections
• 1 pallet • 1" wood screws
• Heavy-duty wall-mounted hose rack • (5) coat hooks
• 3" deck screws

TIME: 45 MINUTES **DIFFICULTY:** MEDIUM

Organizing gardening tools is even more of a challenge than tidying up your general tool collection or a set of woodworking tools. The problem is that gardening calls for both long- and short-handled tools (and even some medium-length-handled tools, like a garden spade). That creates special challenges. Even if you own a garden shed where you can keep your tools out of view, the chances are that those tools are a jumble inside the shed. Getting them organized in one place can seem like an overwhelming nightmare.

You can certainly buy pricey wall hangers and storage features for your gardening equipment. Aside from the expense, those features don't really allow for the type of customization you need. Every gardener tends to use a different collection of tools; you need an all-in-one storage unit that will provide for every implement you use. This project is the answer to that need.

With room for long-handled tools like shovels and rakes and storage tubes for smaller, yet no less essential standards like a garden trowel, this organizer will keep your collection of gardening gear neat as a pin and ready for use.

The project involves a lot of cutting and separating deck boards from stringers. Be patient and use the right tools for these jobs and you should have no problem fabricating the structure in a long afternoon. Then it's just a matter of hanging it on a fence, shed, or even a house wall near where you do most of your gardening.

HOW YOU MAKE IT

1. Cut three pieces of the 2" PVC pipe 5" long. Strip the bottom boards off the pallet using a frameless hacksaw or reciprocating saw.

2. Carefully cut the middle stringer 26" in from one end, using a circular saw. Separate the 26" portion from the top deck boards using a frameless hacksaw or reciprocating saw and remove.

3. Reattach two bottom deck boards: one with its outer edge aligned with the cut edge of the middle stringer, and the other at the end of the pallet with the uncut middle stringer still attached.

4. Measure and mark the long-handled tool slot hole on the outside face of both outside stringers. The first hole is centered 3" in from the end where the middle stringer was removed. The second hole is centered 9" from the first, and the third is centered 12" from the second. All three holes should be centered 2" in from the outside edge of the stringers (the side with the top deck boards still attached).

5. Drill out each hole with a 2" Forstner bit, centered on the marks. Clamp a sacrificial board underneath to prevent tear out. Finish the slots by cutting into them with a jigsaw, on the side opposite the top deck boards.

6. Drill large access holes all the way through the pipe sections, holding them in a vise, to allow drill or driver access to attach them. Use 1" wood screws to screw the PVC pipe sections to the ends of the outside stringers and deck boards in three places.

7. Screw the wall-mounted hose rack to one end of the end deck board on the side opposite the top deck boards. Screw the five coat hooks to what will be the front of the rack, on the two deck boards, spaced evenly to allow for tools to hang without interfering with one another.

8. Screw the tool organizer to a fence or wall, attaching it to either studs or fence rails. Finish as desired (you can also leave it natural).

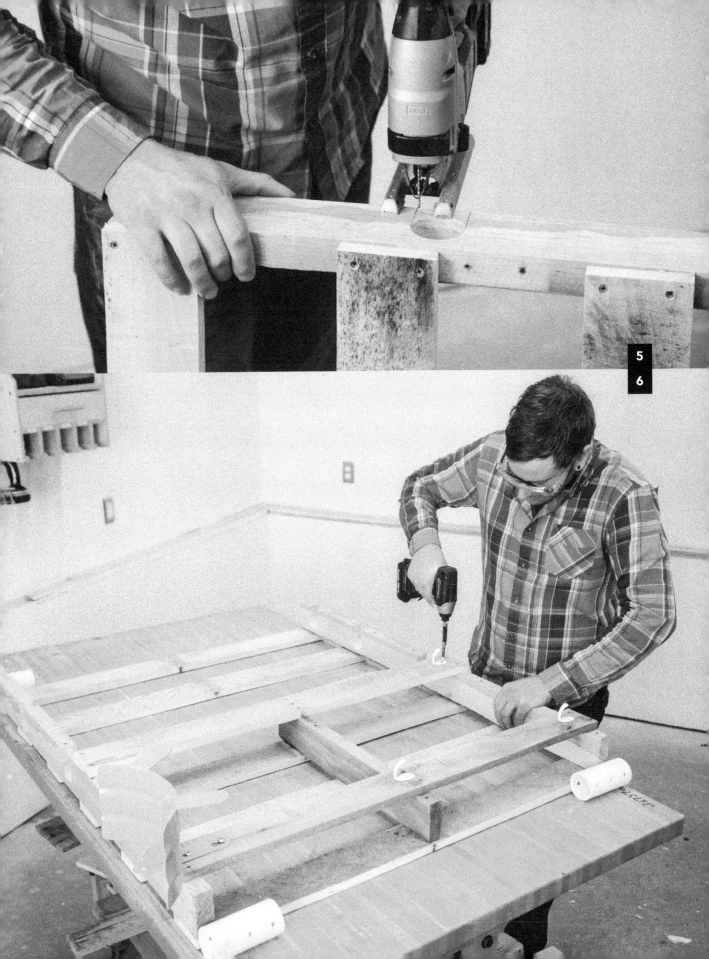

SMALL WALL-MOUNTED SHELF

Sometimes smaller is better. If all you need is a small display shelf for curios, collections, small pictures, or knickknacks, a full-size bookshelf would not only be overkill, it would be wasted space.

That's where this small display shelf comes in. It's compact enough that it won't get in the way of foot traffic, even in a hall or other confined quarters. It's simple enough to build and so basic in design that you may be able to construct it with leftovers from other pallet projects. Fortunately, though, it's sturdy enough to display even heavy items.

The shelf shown here has been finished natural, which allows whatever's stored on the shelves to grab all the attention. But you could just as easily paint it to suit your home's interior, and even accent it with stencils or a little freehand brushwork to show your artistic side.

HOW YOU MAKE IT

1. Use a circular saw to cut the top deck boards of a pallet along one edge of the central stringer. Cut the remaining two-stringer section 21" long.

2. Remove all the top deck boards on the stringer section. Remove the bottom deck boards, leaving the end board and the one on the other side of the notch.

3. Cut two of the removed deck boards 20 ³/₄" long. Screw each onto one end of the stringers with 3" wood screws (the boards should be flush with the stringers).

4. Cut a shelf 17 ³/₄" long from a deck board. Measure and mark 12" up from one end of the frame. Hold the shelf in position and drill pilot holes from outside into the shelf edges. Drill pilot holes and nail the shelf in place with 2" casing nails. (If the deck boards you've reclaimed are too thin for this, you can mount the shelf with metal L brackets—just make sure the shelf is level.)

5. Use a stud finder to locate the studs where you want to hang the shelf. Drill mounting holes through the back boards. Putty all the screwheads, let dry, and sand the shelf. Finish it natural with a polyurethane sealer. Screw the shelf to the studs with 3" wood screws.

LARGE SHOE RACK

This three-shelf unit was designed for a mudroom. It's meant to save you the money on a retail shoe stand, while offering the kind of adaptability you'd be hard-pressed to find at retail. The top shelf can be used as a bench if you keep this in a mudroom—just add a bench cushion.

The dimensions involve basic straight cuts and should be very easy to adapt to the space you have available. Make it taller, thinner, or wider to suit your storage needs. You can also make multiples because they can easily be stacked. You can even hang one or more on a mudroom wall or inside a larger closet.

The versatility doesn't stop there. You don't need to use this "shoe stand" for shoes. It can just as easily accommodate books, sweaters, or folded pants. No matter what you use it for, you can leave it natural for a more rustic appeal or paint it to fit in with your current decor.

Although they are incredibly useful, earning their keep within minutes of being installed, simple shoe stands are often overlocked as mudroom additions or accents in a bedroom closet. That's a shame because they are key to keeping clutter in line. Left without a place to go, shoes in an entry hall or bedroom jumble into a pile on the floor that becomes just another tripping hazard. But add a sturdy shoe stand of the right size and your shoes will be appealingly organized—and may even last longer in the bargain.

WHAT YOU'LL NEED

TOOLS:
Pry bar or pallet buster • Frameless hacksaw or reciprocating saw • Measuring tape • Carpenter's pencil • Circular saw or table saw • Power drill and bits • Putty knife (optional) • Paintbrush (optional)

MATERIALS:
2 pallets • 2½" flathead wood screws • (12) 2" corner brackets • 1" flathead wood screws • Wood putty (optional) • 80-grit sandpaper (optional) • Paint or finish (optional) • 4 adjustable screw-in feet (optional)

CUT LIST:
(4) 2 x 4 x 26½" stringer legs • (4) 2 x 4 x 26½" stringer rails • 1 x 4 x 11½" deck board shelf planks

TIME: 1 HOUR   **DIFFICULTY:** MEDIUM

HOW YOU MAKE IT

1. Disassemble two pallets completely using a pry bar and frameless hacksaw. With a measuring tape and circular saw, measure and cut the pieces from the pallets to the dimensions on the cut list.

2. Lay a stringer rail flat across two stringer legs laid on their faces and parallel to one another so that the ends of the rail align with the outside edges of the legs. Locate the rail 2" up from the end of each leg. Screw the rail to the legs at each end with 2½" flathead wood screws.

3. Measure up 7" on the legs from the first rail and mark for the bottom of the middle rail. Screw it in place as you did the first.

4. Align the top rail across the two legs, flush at the two ends along the top. Screw it in place to the legs using 2½" flathead wood screws. Repeat the process, fastening three rails to the remaining two posts.

5. Screw three rails onto the second side of one of the leg pairs, in the same location as the rails on the other side.

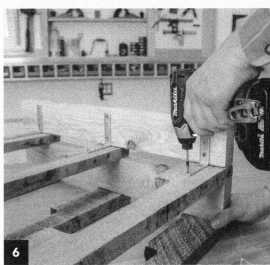

6. Fasten the second leg pair to the first, aligned with the rails on one side, using 2" corner brackets. Use one per end on each rail.

7. Dry lay the deck boards in place across the top. Because this is the most visible surface, the top should use the nicest-looking deck boards. Depending on how varied the widths of your deck boards are, you will likely have to rip one or more deck boards to fit the layout.

8. When the deck boards fit the space perfectly, drill pilot holes and screw each deck board down to the leg ends, using 1" flathead wood screws. Repeat the entire process to install the deck boards on the two lower shelves.

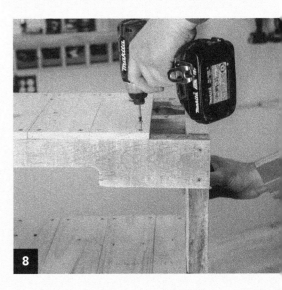

9. If you're painting the shoe stand, putty over the screwheads and sand them smooth. If you find the stand rocks, add adjustable screw-type feet to the bottom of each leg.

HANGING POT RACK

WHAT YOU'LL NEED

TOOLS:
Pry bar or hammer
• Circular saw
• Speed square
• Power drill and
bits • Palm sander
(optional) • Stud
finder

MATERIALS:
1 pallet • 3" wood
screws • Sandpaper
(optional) • Paint or
stain (optional)
• 4" zinc ceiling hooks
• 3" zinc ceiling hooks
• 4 lengths of 2/0
zinc chain

TIME: 30 MINUTES **DIFFICULTY:** EASY

If you've ever clanked your way through pots or pans in a drawer looking for just the right sauté pan, you'll know that these essential cookware items are some of the most difficult kitchen tools to store. That doesn't have to be the case though; there's plenty of room overhead.

Hanging a pot rack from your ceiling is not only a way to organize pots and pans in an at-a-glance fashion; it also makes some of the most-used equipment in the kitchen much more conveniently accessible. All that, and it frees up lots of drawer space for your other kitchen necessities.

It's also a great look that pretty much advertises "an avid cook works here." The rack in this project is finished with a natural appearance common to most wooden pot racks, because the look of the wood so perfectly complements the rugged nature of steel and cast-iron cookware. That said, you can certainly paint

the rack if you prefer. Just be aware that dirt, dust, and smoke all float up in the kitchen—maybe more so than you realize. If you opt for a glossy white finish, or other bright color, you'll have to plan on regular cleanings.

This is a simple rack to build and even simpler to adapt. It may be that you have a smaller kitchen, or just an oddly shaped room. That's okay; you can make this design narrower, shorter, or just plain smaller, and it will still be super useful. In any case, take your time in deciding on a height to hang the rack; it should be at the ideal height for the person who cooks most in the kitchen. If you're worried about support, you can reinforce the hanging connection by installing the cleats described in the Porch Swing project on page 33 and using longer, thicker ceiling screw eyes.

HANGING OUT

Where and how you hang your pot rack is a matter of heading off any potential problems while making the rack as convenient as possible for the cooks who use the kitchen most. Here are some guidelines for trouble-free pot hanging:

● **AVOID THE TEMPTATION TO HANG THE POT RACK NEAR A WINDOW.** There will be some degree of swing in any hanging pot rack as you remove and replace cookware, and a swinging cast iron pan can easily smash a window.

● **ALTHOUGH WE'VE SPECIFIED THAT THE RACK SHOULD BE MOUNTED LOW ENOUGH FOR THE SHORTEST COOK IN THE KITCHEN TO REACH, THAT ONLY** **HOLDS TRUE IF THE RACK HAS BEEN MOUNTED OVER A SURFACE SUCH AS A COUNTER.** If the rack hangs over open floor space, you'll want to adjust it so that the bottoms of the pans are high enough for the tallest user of the kitchen to pass under them. The shorter cook can use a folding step stool to reach the cookware.

● **WHENEVER POSSIBLE, HANG THE RACK OVER A KITCHEN ISLAND, A STOVE, OR SOME OTHER SURFACE,** because a falling pot or pan could hurt anyone standing under the rack and could easily damage a tile or laminate kitchen floor.

HOW YOU MAKE IT

1. Remove the bottom deck boards from a pallet and cut the top boards to one edge of the center stringer so that the rack is two stringers wide. Cut the stringers 24 ¾" from one end. Depending on board placement, this may involve removing a board or ripping it to suit. You may also want to cut the stringers from each end to center the notches, if any.

2. Use a speed square to mark a 45° miter on the ends of the stringers, narrowing the stringers toward the open side. Make the cuts with a circular saw.

3. Cut a center brace 21 ¾" long, from the third waste stringer. Place the brace face down between the two rack stringers, centered along their length. Screw the stringers to the brace ends with 3" wood screws.

4. Sand or distress the rack as desired, and paint or finish it. (The rack shown here was left natural.)

5. Screw 4" ceiling hooks 14" to 16" apart and centered along the top edge of each stringer. Screw 3" ceiling hooks to the bottom faces of the deck boards (now the underside of the pot rack). Position one hook at each end of each deck board, screwing it up into a stringer. Center

a hook along the length of center brace. If your deck boards are ¾" or thicker, you can add more screw hooks.

6. Use a stud finder to mark ceiling joist locations. Screw 4" ceiling hooks into the ceiling joists and use lengths of 2/0 chain to hang the rack from the ceiling.

Alternative: If hanging the rack from a wall, use a stud finder to mark stud location. Screw one side of the rack to the wall with 3" wood screws. Screw 4" ceiling hooks to the same studs at the top of the wall, and run the chain between the wall hooks and the outside stringer hooks.

POT-HANGING OPTIONS & ALTERNATIVES

The project here is amazingly adaptable to your own circumstances and the available space and configuration in your kitchen. Be creative when considering how you might want to mount or modify this pot hanger.

● **IT'S NOT JUST FOR POTS AND PANS!** Use the hooks in the face of the deck boards—or anywhere, for that matter—to support utensils. Having the right spatula nearby and ready for use can be indispensable, and, arguably, most cooks use utensils even more than they use their cookware. Of course, if you really want to vary the look or get the most out of your pot hanger, add a row of smaller hooks for coffee mugs or beer steins.

Rounded ends add flair to a wall-mounted pot hanger made from deconstructed pallet boards. The dark stain helps hide flaws and imperfections, and makes the perfect foil for copper pans.

● **GO SMALL.** Have a galley kitchen or similar small space? You can modify the pot hanger in this project to suit. You might even want to simply mount a single stringer on edge to your ceiling joists with countersunk six-inch lag screws, and then line the stringer bottom edge with hooks. For a longer hanger, butt two stringers together.

● **GO WALL.** Although we've included a half-wall-mounted option in the instructions for this project, you can take the idea one step further. In the simplest sense, you can screw the pot hanger as it is (without the ceiling hooks on top) directly to wall studs and then hang pots and pans from the hooks that project out horizontally. You can also deconstruct a pallet and form your own custom hanger from different pieces, secured to the wall. This is a way to put blank wall space to good use and tailor the look and size of the rack to exactly suit the pots and pans you need to hang.

LARGE BOOKSHELF

WHAT YOU'LL NEED

TOOLS:
Pry bar and hammer • Circular saw • Measuring tape • Carpenter's pencil • Power drill and bits • Level • Hammer • Putty knife • Palm sander • Paintbrush

MATERIALS:
1 pallet • 2" wood screws • Finish nails • Wood putty • 80-grit sandpaper • Primer (optional) • Paint (optional)

TIME: 45 MINUTES **DIFFICULTY:** MEDIUM

Bookshelves are some of the most versatile and just plain handiest pieces of storage furniture in any house. The bookshelf in this project is sized specifically to accommodate books, but it is ideal for storing many objects. Dress it up with paint and perhaps some subtle stenciling, and it can be a wonderful dining room display cabinet for your favorite glassware. Paint different sections in contrasting primary colors and it will fit right into your toddler's bedroom as a vibrant home for toys or your child's favorite illustrated books. Or go with a more understated stain or natural finish and use the bookshelf in your home office to keep office supplies in order and within arm's reach.

No matter what you use it for, this bookshelf will bring a handsome look to any room. The split sides are a slightly craftsman-style touch, forming a stable base on which the bookshelf stands. The fascia boards that front the shelves hide the shelf brackets and give the unit a lovely finished look. For ease of fabrication, and to create a visual back for the bookshelves, the deck boards have been left attached to the stringer pair that forms the back legs of the bookshelf. The deck boards could be removed with the help of a reciprocating saw to give the bookshelves a more conventional appearance—but think twice about doing that. The deck boards add a lot of stability and will keep the bookshelves square over time. They can also be ideal for securing the bookshelf to a wall for added stability.

One of the most wonderful things about this bookshelf is that—like most pieces of pallet furniture—it's very adaptable. Have a bigger library of books? Make a wider bookshelf by using a full pallet of three stringers (don't remove the central stringer—it will keep the shelves from sagging under the load of heavy books). Want to go more vertical? Stack a second pallet bookshelf unit on top (see "Safe Stacking" below). Another excellent trait of this unit is that it is entirely portable, and you'll find it easy to move wherever you need it.

You can also switch up the design, as you prefer. Rip and cut a deck board to fill in the vertical gap on each side if you prefer a "closed" bookshelf. Although the bookshelf in this project has been painted yellow, it would look handsome painted white or a neutral color. If you're using it in a more colorful or funky setting, you can paint it with different colors for the legs and the shelves, or one bright color with stenciled designs down the legs. Ultimately, the choice is to finish it to blend in or stand out, but keep in mind that rows of books are a wonderful visual that stands out all on their own.

SAFE STACKING

The beauty of a bookshelf like the one in this project is that it can be stacked to create a taller unit with double the capacity. But any time you stack individual bookshelf units, it's important to ensure the structure is entirely safe. You don't want to find out it's unstable after you have filled it with heavy books.

Given the variable thicknesses of the deck boards from different pallets, it's wise to permanently fix a stacked unit to the lower bookshelf with horizontal cleats screwed across the joint where the top rests on the bottom. You can attach the cleats on the inside or outside, but they will actually look better on the outside of the bookshelves and will not take up real estate that could be used by books.

You should also secure stacked bookshelves to the wall. There are many ways to do this; you'll find solutions such as security straps at hardware stores and home centers, or you can simply screw the bookshelves to the wall by driving screws through the back deck boards and into wall studs.

In any case, avoid stacking shelves in areas of heavy traffic flow, where people will often bump the bookcases.

Also follow common-sense rules for how you place books on the shelves. Ideally, heavier books, such as coffee table volumes, go on the bottom. Lighter paperbacks should be placed on the top shelves.

HOW YOU MAKE IT

1. Remove the bottom deck boards from a pallet and use a circular saw to cut the top deck boards along one edge of the middle stringer.

2. Set the two-stringer section on its side (resting on a stringer face). Cut two 4 ½" spacers from scrap. Use the spacers to separate the stringer resting on the surface and a separate deconstructed stringer laid parallel to the first (any notches should face each other).

3. Measure and mark shelf locations, starting with the first 8" up from the bottom. Make subsequent marks across both stringers at 21 ½", 34 ½", and 47 ¼". These marks represent the top edges of the shelf cleats.

4. Cut and rip eight shelf cleats 1 ¾" wide by 10 ½" long from stringers. Align the top edge of the first cleat with the 8" line so that the back edge is flush with the back of the rear stringer (the stringer with the deck boards attached). Screw the cleat across the stringers with 2" wood screws. Repeat the process with cleats at the remaining three marks.

5. Lay the bookshelves on the opposite side and repeat the process to construct the second bookshelf side. Stand the bookshelf up and check for level and plumb. Adjust the stringer legs as necessary.

6. Check level across the brackets and adjust as necessary. Starting at the top, dry lay three shelf boards 17 ¾" long, cut from deck boards, across the top cleats (there should be a gap at the front of the shelves). Drill pilot holes and fasten the shelves to the cleats with finish nails. Repeat to install the rest of the shelves.

7. Rip four 2 ½ x 17 ¾" fascia boards from deck boards. Drill pilot holes and fasten the fascia boards in front of the shelves by nailing them to the shelf boards and cleats.

8. Putty over all the nail heads, let dry, and sand smooth. Sand the entire bookshelf, finish natural, or prime and paint in the desired color.

STYLING YOUR BOOKSHELF

If you've gone to the trouble to build a handsome bookshelf, it's a shame to haphazardly pile books on the shelves or just line them up in boring rows. Use the strategies below to spruce up the look of the bookshelves and add visual interest to any room.

● STACK BOOKS VERTICALLY AND HORIZONTALLY.

Piles of books can serve as bookends or just break up long, boring rows of books. This is also a good way to store books that are too tall to fit into the shelves vertically.

● TOP STACKED BOOKS WITH A CANDLE OR OTHER EYE-CATCHING BRIC-A-BRAC.

This will add even more zest to the look.

● INTERSPERSE BOOKS AND PHOTOS. This

is a great way to show off photos, even if they've been framed for wall hanging, because you can simply lean them against the back of the bookshelf. For an even more stylish look, dare to lean a small photo in front of the book spines.

● INCORPORATE KEEPSAKE BOXES AS HEAVY DECORATIVE ADDITIONS THAT ALSO SERVE A STORAGE PURPOSE. These

can be used to hide away small items like pens, office supplies, and other items that wouldn't necessarily improve the look of the shelves. Match the material of the box—metal, cardboard, wood, or brightly colored plastic—to the look of the shelves.

● DON'T BE AFRAID OF BLANK SPACES.

Leaving a strategic gap can be a way of adding a little elegance to the bookshelf. Any gap shouldn't be more than a few inches wide or it risks looking like wasted space.

QUICK 3

Small storage fixtures can have a big impact when they're used in the right places to add ease and comfort to daily living. The truth is, most people don't think to buy simple items like mug holders and coasters. They just tolerate the inefficiencies, constantly tripping over towels on the bathroom floor that simply don't have a place on the wall or putting up with water rings on their lovely coffee table. It's a shame, because these small annoyances are so easily avoidable. What's more, crafting these small amenities is almost instantaneous gratification. You'll save a little bit of money, but you'll also be pleasantly surprised at how much your modest creations get used. One of the best things about small projects such as these, however, is that you can customize them to your heart's delight. It's a small matter to put your own signature on a set of coasters, and if you come up with a really cool look, go ahead and whip out multiples for some wonderful, handmade Christmas gifts. In any case, these three super-simple projects are all exceedingly easy and can be fabricated in minutes. Those may be the best minutes you spend in your workshop.

1. TOWEL LADDER RACK

Stock bathroom towel racks are notoriously undersized, especially for today's common beach towel–size plush bathroom linens. The answer? Use the vertical space to its best advantage by creating a towel "ladder" rack. Towels are essentially hung in a layered way that is most space efficient. A pallet is ideal for these types of racks, especially if you're building one for a small or narrow bathroom. Start by cutting all the deck boards along one edge of a pallet's center stringer. Remove all the bottom deck boards, and then cut the stringers about eight inches long, leaving one deck board in place between the end and the cuts. Cut other racks—as many as you need for the number of towels you want to hang—to the same length. Measure and mark a hole centered both ways on the outside of each stringer and use a spade bit to drill a three-quarter-inch hole on each side. Cut a three-quarter-inch dowel to length and tap it through the holes. Sand the rack all over, prime it, and paint it gloss white or a gloss color to complement or match your bathroom wall color. Mount the rack or racks on studs, with two-inch wood screws driven through the underside of the deck board sixteen inches on center (drill pilot holes first).

2. MUG HOLDER

All too often, homeowners waste precious cabinet space storing chunky mugs where they're likely to get bumped around and eventually broken. Because mugs usually make interesting visuals and are used so often, it makes sense to get them out and close to where they will be needed. That means a mug holder, and a wall-mounted unit will be the most space-efficient option. To make one quickly and easily, remove the deck boards from the bottom of a pallet and cut along one side of the center stringer. Cut the stringers in from one end to a distance that includes two deck boards. Use one of the deck boards from the longer portion as a shelf screwed across the uncut ends of the stringers. Sand the holder all over and paint it white, or in a color that complements your kitchen color (or leave it natural if you have a country kitchen). Screw stainless steel cup hooks in your favorite style to the underside of the deck boards and mount the holder on a wall by driving two-inch screws through the deck boards and into studs.

3. DRINK COASTERS

These simple, quick, and easy-to-make eye-catchers are not only a great addition to your home, they also make fantastic gifts. Cut three-and-a-half-inch squares from deck boards and sand them well. Make a pattern of small indentations with a drill to create visual interest and wick away any moisture, or cut a light circle into the surface of each coaster with a hole saw. Then finish or paint as desired, using matte paint or stain. The variations you can create are almost endless. Cut different shapes such as hexagons by using a jigsaw instead of a hole saw. Or use a jigsaw to cut each coaster into a unique oval or other unusual shape. You can paint the coasters in vibrant colors, but it makes more sense to stain them and avoid any sealing finishes—the coaster should be left porous to absorb liquids and condensation. You can also stencil witty images or even words onto each coaster for a truly unique look.

SPICE RACK

WHAT YOU'LL NEED

TOOLS:
Circular saw or table saw
• Speed square • Measuring
tape • Carpenter's pencil
• Bar clamp • Power drill and
bits • Hammer • Sanding
block • 2" paintbrush
• Torpedo level

MATERIALS:
1 pallet • 2" finish nails
• Wood putty • 100-grit
sandpaper • Stain or
paint

TIME: 20 MINUTES **DIFFICULTY:** EASY

Everybody has one. That one shelf in a cupboard where you keep spices, many of which you don't even realize you have. They're jammed in, one in front of the other, making finding the spice you need a matter of pulling every single spice jar out of the cupboard—and then putting them all back again once you're done.

That's why the ideal place for spices is in a rack where it's easy to see the jar you need and all the jars are kept neat, tidy, and organized. In other words, a rack like the one in this project.

This is a small project that requires a good bit of sawing, but is otherwise not a challenge to assemble. However, the measurements do need to be precise in such a small construction. Errors can quickly be magnified, so be careful as you work.

The rack is meant to be screwed to a wall, but it will also sit comfortably under a cabinet on a countertop. The idea is always to make the spices as conveniently located as possible for wherever you do most of your cooking or baking.

This rack has been stained, but you may prefer to paint yours white or leave it natural. Before choosing how you're going to finish it, consider that something this small on a wall in the kitchen is really a design accent. Don't be afraid to experiment with brighter colors that complement the existing color scheme in your kitchen.

HOW YOU MAKE IT

1. Deconstruct a pallet. Cut two sides 19 ½" long from stringers, and two back braces 13" long from deck boards. Cut a 13" top and bottom from stringers.

2. Lay the two sides next to each other on their faces so that they are perfectly aligned. Use a speed square to make a mark on each board 6 ¼" from the bottom end of the side pieces and another 6 ¼" up from that mark.

3. Clamp the sides to the top so that the top is flush on both ends. Drill pilot holes and fasten the sides to the top with finish nails.

4. Lay one back brace under the top, flat between the sides. Lay the second with its top edge aligned with the first mark up from the bottom. Drill pilot holes through the sides into the edges of the braces and nail the sides to the braces with finish nails.

5. Rip and cut three shelves 2 ¾" wide by 13" long from deck boards. Rip and cut three fronts from stringers, 1 ½" wide. Position the bottom flush with the bottom of the sides. Position the other two shelves flush with the shelf marks (the back edges of all three should be flush with the backs of the sides). Fasten them in place as you did the top.

6. Nail the shelf fronts perpendicular to the shelves, with the front boards' bottom edges flush with the bottom of the shelves.

7. Conceal the nail heads with wood putty, let it dry, and sand the unit all over before painting it (or staining it if you prefer). Choose a location, and drive screws through the back boards into studs or anchors, checking to ensure level before tightening them all the way down.

CRAFTS CENTER

Don't let the name of this project fool you; this can also be a wonderful organizer for all your gift-wrapping supplies. You know, all those rolls of wrapping paper and bags of bows that are probably jumbled together in a closet somewhere. The Crafts Center will not only make wrapping presents easier and quicker, but it might also make that particular task fun.

The unit has been designed with three handy rods meant to hang standard rolls of craft or wrapping paper right where you need them. But these rods can just as easily accommodate rolls of ribbon, tape, or even decorative twine or cord. Your loose crafting supplies can be kept in cups on the shelves, while extra rolls of paper can be slid into the long paper holder alongside the shelves. Add hooks to the front of the two horizontal deck boards to hold scissors or other crafting tools or modify the structure however you want to best serve your own crafty needs.

This project has been left unfinished for a simple and attractive workmanlike appearance, but it's an easy job to paint the organizer to match or complement your crafting room. Just make sure you mount it on studs, because it's sizable and the pallet stocked with supplies can be weighty.

It's a fact of homeownership that one of the least tidy areas in the whole house is destined to be wherever crafts are done. Creativity just seems to spawn mess, but clutter in a workspace can make you less productive and make the space—usually an area where you nurture your passion for one pastime or another—less inviting. Never fear, pallets are here to get you (or your loved one) squared away!

WHAT YOU'LL NEED

TOOLS:
Measuring tape • Carpenter's pencil • Circular saw or table saw • Pry bar or pallet buster • Frameless hacksaw or reciprocating saw • Power drill and bits • Level • Palm sander • Putty knife (optional) • Paintbrush (optional)

MATERIALS:
2 x 4" pine • 1¼"-diameter wood dowel • 1 pallet • 3" flathead wood screws • (6) open U closet rod brackets • 2" flathead wood screws • 80-grit sandpaper • Wood putty (optional) • Paint or finish (optional)

CUT LIST:
(1) 1½ x 3½ x 35½" short shelf • (1) 1½ x 3½ x 37" long shelf • (1) ¾ x 3½ x 20¾" top • (3) 1¼ x 36½" wood dowel wrapping paper hangers

TIME: 1 HOUR **DIFFICULTY:** MEDIUM

HOW YOU MAKE IT

1. With a measuring tape and circular saw, measure and cut the shelves from the pine board and the dowels to the dimensions listed on the cut list. Using a pry bar and frameless hacksaw, remove the deck boards from the bottom of the pallet, being careful to keep them intact. Remove the top deck boards 16" from one end.

2. Cut the center stringer 14½" from the end that you just removed the top deck boards from. Fasten the long shelf in place by screwing the two side stringers to the shelf ends, and the shelf to the cut end of the middle stringer, using 3" wood screws. Note: Check the shelf for level before driving the screws.

3. Measure 13½" up from the shelf and mark the inside of the center and side stringer. Position the short shelf with its bottom aligned on the marks. Screw each stringer to a shelf end.

4. Screw a rod bracket to the inside face of each side stringer so that the bottom of the bracket is flush with the end of the stringer. Slip a dowel into the brackets and measure up 3" on each side from the top of the dowel. Position the second set of brackets with their bottoms flush with the marks and screw them in place. Repeat with a third set of brackets.

5. Fasten a deck board across the stringers 1" up from the long shelf by drilling pilot holes and screwing the deck board to the stringer with 2" wood screws. Repeat the process with a deck board 1" up from the short shelf.

6. Drill pilot holes and screw the deck board top across the ends of the center and side stringers, directly up from the short shelf.

7. Lightly sand the unit all over with a palm sander. If you're painting the Crafts Center, putty over the screw heads and sand smooth, then prime and paint the color of your choice. You can stain the unit if you prefer, but the shelves will likely wind up a different tone than the rest of the wood.

8. Measure and mark the back deck boards for the mounting screws 16" on center (two screws in at least three separate boards, spaced evenly top to bottom). Mount the Crafts Center to the wall studs with at least six screws in the final location.

5
6

WINE AND LIQUOR BOTTLE RACK

WHAT YOU'LL NEED

TOOLS:
Circular saw • Measuring tape • Pry bar • Carpenter's pencil • Jigsaw • Palm sander • Power drill and bits • Level • Paintbrush • Stud finder

MATERIALS:
1 pallet • Grid paper • Cardboard • 80-grit sandpaper • 3" wood screws • Bolt and nut • 10" length of ⅜" chain • Walnut stain • Wood putty

TIME: 20 MINUTES   **DIFFICULTY:** EASY

In this age of the wine box, if you're buying and storing wine bottles, you might as well show them off. And what better way to do that then to build a wonderfully rustic rack that juxtaposes the sleek, sophisticated look of wine bottles (or the subtle colorations of liquor bottles) against the earthy appeal of pallet wood.

It's a simple rack to build; the hardest part is making the curving cut in the three stringers of the pallet, but that's also a chance for even more creativity. You can create a simple curving pattern as with this rack, create one more involved, or even settle on a more geometric approach for a modern look. Of course,

if you're not comfortable with a jigsaw, you can always just miter the stringers from the front edge of the rail back to the mounting boards.

You can also vary the look of the rack. Although we've distressed and stained the rack shown here (to capture the charm of a vineyard barrel), you can certainly finish it natural for a more understated approach. If you're a little crafty, you can even stencil a fun saying or other words on the front of the rack, or paint the whole thing in an eye-catching color scheme. Just be done by cocktail hour!

HOW YOU MAKE IT

1. Use a circular saw to cut the stringers of a pallet 13" from one end, or to the inside edge of the third top deck board from the end.

2. Remove all but the end bottom deck board (the top deck boards will serve as the back of the wine rack). Work out a curved pattern for the stringer faces on a piece of grid paper. Transfer the design to a piece of cardboard and cut it out to create a template.

3. Use the template to trace the cutting lines on the face of each stringer. Cut along the lines with a jigsaw, and sand the surfaces after you're done.

4. Screw a deck board to the uncut ends of the stringers, using 3" wood screws. Secure a bolt and nut at the end of a small length of chain and whip the chain, alternating ends, against the surface of the wood, focusing on the stringers. Don't hit the wood so hard that you break any member—the goal is to convincingly distress the surface.

5. Stain the wood with a walnut stain as used here, or similar stain, to enhance the distressed appearance.

6. Once the stain has dried, use a stud finder to locate and mark the studs on the wall to which the rack will be mounted. Use a helper to hold the rack up to the desired height, and check for level.

7. Drill and countersink mounting holes for 3" wood screws, and screw the rack to the wall, checking level again before tightening the screws. Dab wood putty over the screw heads and, when dry, sand and dab with stain.

BEER CADDY

As any self-respecting weekend warrior knows, it's good to keep your beers handy because you never know when you might need a fresh brew. That's especially true on trips to the lake or even a lazy afternoon in the backyard. This caddy is an ideal way to keep your stash of suds on hand and ready for consumption—all without worrying that the bottles will get bumped around and possibly broken.

This caddy takes little expertise and time and can be constructed from odds and ends left over from other pallet projects. The construction is intentionally designed to be rough and tumble so that it fits right into a wooded shore next to your favorite fishing hole and can be tossed into the bed of a pickup truck when empty.

WHAT YOU'LL NEED

TOOLS:
Pry bar or pallet buster • Frameless hacksaw or reciprocating saw • Circular saw • Power drill and bits • Palm sander • Paintbrush (optional) • Measuring tape • Carpenter's pencil

MATERIALS:
1 pallet • 3" deck screws • 1" stainless steel wood screws • 80-grit sandpaper • Paint or stain (optional) • Steel wall-mount bottle opener • 3" gate handle

CUT LIST:
(1) 1½ x 3½ x 15" stringer bottom
• (2) 1½ x 3½ x 16½" stringer sides
• (1) 1½ x 2 x 15" stringer top
• (4) ¾ x 3½ x 18" deck board rails
• (1) ¾ x 3½ x 15" deck board rail

TIME: 45 MINUTES **DIFFICULTY:** EASY

3

4

HOW YOU MAKE IT

1. Disassemble the pallet completely using a pry bar and frameless hacksaw. With a circular saw, cut the stringers and deck boards to the lengths listed on the cut list. *Note: The pallet used for this project came with stringer notches. If the pallet you're working with doesn't, you can leave the sides of the caddy a uniform width (and eliminate ripping the top to suit) or, for more design flair, clip the top corners of the side boards so that the clipped end is 2" wide.*

2. Position the unnotched end of one side board flush to one end of the bottom and screw it to the bottom with 3" deck screws. Repeat with the opposite side.

3. Position the top between the inside faces of the notched side boards and screw it in place.

4. Center the shorter deck board rail on one of the longer ones, with the top and bottom edges aligned. Screw it to the longer board with 1" wood screws.

5. Drill pilot holes and screw the deck board rails on the front and back edges of the stringer sides. The rails should be positioned about ½" above the top of the bottom. The "filler" board on the back deck board rail should sit inside the caddy, as a buffer for the bottles.

6. Sand all over and finish the caddy as desired. Screw the bottle opener to one side at the top. Measure and mark the center across the length of the caddy's top and screw the handle in place.

TOOL CARRIER

This design is based on the traditional carpenter's tool box. It is meant to carry larger, more awkward tools or a great number of smaller tools. There is an abundance of space inside, making this a great choice for the avid craftsperson—either an experienced woodworker or a general DI'Yer who tackles a lot of diverse projects.

The construction is a bit unorthodox and was developed to make best use of boards reclaimed from a deconstructed pallet. You may even be able to build it with leftovers from another pallet wood project. However, some pallets have notched stringers. In that case, you may be forced to use standard two-by-fours for the bottom boards; notched stringers can still be cut in creative ways to accommodate both the posts and the end boards.

Obviously, this is a workhorse. As such, there's really no point to finishing it because hopefully it will get banged around and see a lot of rugged use. Depending on how rough-and-tumble that use is (for instance, if the caddy is going to be bouncing around the bed of a pickup truck all day), you may want to reinforce the corners and secure the top and bottom frames together.

WHAT YOU'LL NEED

TOOLS:
Pry bar or pallet buster • Frameless hacksaw or reciprocating saw • Circular saw • Jigsaw • Power drill and bits • Measuring tape • Carpenter's pencil • 1" spade bit • Clamps

MATERIALS:
1 pallet • 3" wood screws • 1"-diameter wood dowel • 2" wood screws

CUT LIST:
(3) 1½ x 3½ x 18" stringer bottoms
• (4) 1½ x 3½ x 10½" stringer ends
• (4) ¾ x 3½ x 21" deck board sides
• 1 x 21" dowel handle
• (2) 1 ½ x 3 ½ x 14" posts

TIME: 1 HOUR **DIFFICULTY:** MEDIUM

HOW YOU MAKE IT

1. Disassemble the pallet completely using a pry bar and frameless hacksaw, being careful to preserve the wood as much as possible. With a circular saw, cut the deck boards and stringers to the dimensions listed on cut list.

2. Build a basic box frame by using 3" woods screws to fasten two deck board sides to the ends of two stringer end boards (drill pilot holes through the faces of the deck board sides first). Measure diagonals to ensure the frame is square.

3. Attach the sides and the ends to the three bottom boards laid side by side, perfectly flush with one another. Screw the ends to the ends of the bottom boards. Drill pilot holes and screw the deck board sides to the edges of the outside bottom boards.

4. Measure and mark each post 1" in from each side at one end. Measure 3" down from the end on each side and draw a line connecting the end and the edge marks on each side. Make these angle cuts and use this post as a template to mark the second one. Cut the second post the same way.

5. Measure and mark each post for the center of the dowel handle, 2" down from the pointed end and centered side to side. Drill out the holes with a 1" spade bit.

6. Measure and mark the position for the posts on the frame, centered side to side on the ends. Screw the first post in place to the bottom and ends.

7. Slide the dowel handle into the post (you may need to tap it into place). Slide the opposite post onto the other end of the dowel and clamp the post in position. Screw the post to the ends and bottom as you did with the first one.

RECYCLING BIN HOLDER

WHAT YOU'LL NEED

TOOLS:
Prybar or pallet buster
• Frameless hacksaw or
reciprocating saw • Circular
saw • Power drill and bits
• Clamps • Measuring tape
• Carpenter's pencil

MATERIALS:
2 pallets • 3" wood screws
• 2" stainless steel wood screws
or deck screws • 1½" stainless
steel or galvanized wood screws
• 3" gate handle • 24 x 15 1/2"
(or smaller) plastic recycling bin

CUT LIST:
(4) 1½ x 3½ x 21" stringer frame ends
• (4) 1½ x 3½ x 31" stringer frame sides
• (32) ¾ x 3½ x 16" deck board pickets
• (6) ¾ x 3½ x 34" deck board lid boards
• (3) ¾ x 3½ x 21" deck board lid cross braces

TIME: 1 HOUR   DIFFICULTY: MEDIUM

Recycling is a way for you to do your part to better the environment. As landfills get fuller and fuller, and environmental issues become more and more pressing, recycling takes on an increased urgency. Chances are, you have one or two bins to collect your glass and metal waste for pickup. The odds are good that those bins are as unattractive as they are useful. That's where this "bin" comes in (it can more accurately be called a bin shed).

The design of this project is based around a typical municipal recycling bin. Measure yours to ensure that it matches, or revise the design to accommodate a different size. You can even size it to suit a garbage can, but that will probably mean adding a door on one side so that you can easily remove the can on garbage collection day.

In any case, the finished structure is intended to be used outside. That's where most people keep their recyclables, and it's meant to be handy. You can make it even more so by adding a center brace across the inside of one side, and then cutting the boards to create a three-inch-wide opening that you can use as a bottle or can drop slot.

This has been left natural to save time and effort, but if you keep your recycling in a visible location along the house, or just like to have things a little more attractive, you can sand and paint or finish the outside of the bin to match or contrast the home itself. You can even stencil letters or words on it.

HOW YOU MAKE IT

1. Disassemble at least two pallets using a pry bar and frameless hacksaw. Use a circular saw to cut the deck boards and stringers to the dimensions listed on the cut list. Plan for any notches to fall in the middle of the length of any piece to avoid problems with screwing surfaces.

2. Build the top frame by butt joining two ends to two sides. Dry fit the frame and measure the angles to ensure square. Use 3" wood screws at each joint, driving them through the end boards into the ends of the sides. Repeat to build the second frame.

3. Clamp the frames in position so that you can attach the boards for one end. Start with the outside boards. They should align with the outside edges of the frames, flush at one end with a frame bottom, and projecting 1½" above the top edge of the opposite frame. When you're sure the boards are positioned exactly perpendicular to the frames, drill pilot holes and screw them to the frame's top and bottom with 2" stainless steel wood screws or deck screws.

4. Dry position the remaining boards for the end, spacing them as necessary. Drill pilot holes and screw the boards to the frames.

Flip the frame and repeat the process with the opposite end.

Optional: At this point, you cut measure and cut floor boards for the inside of the bin if you prefer to have a solid floor on which to place the recycling bin.

5. With the frames sitting on their sides, repeat the process, except that the end boards project ¾" out from the edges of the frames, covering the edges of the end boards.

6. Place and space the remaining side deck boards. Drill pilot holes and screw them in place with the 2" screws. Flip and screw the deck boards in place on the opposite side.

7. Place the lid boards in position on top of the top frame to ensure they fit inside the space for the lid. Remove the boards and lay out the lid on a smooth, level work surface. Screw the frame pieces down to the lid boards with 1½" stainless steel or galvanized wood screws.

8. Measure and mark the center side to side of the lid's center cross brace and screw the handle in place. Determine where you'll place the bin and level the surface if it is a dirt area. Set it in place, put the recycling bin inside, and cover with the lid.

CHAPTER FOUR

HOME GOODS (AND GREATS!)

Anybody who has ever shelled out money for even a moderately nice platform bed or picture frame knows just how pricey home furnishings, storage fixtures, and decorative items can be.

It's easy to blow a budget just getting your hands on essential furnishings that you'll need to be comfortable in your home. But no more. Now you can build most of what you need with a little time, a modest amount of expertise, and some careful attention to deals. Oh, and a few pallets!

This is where pallet creations can have a big impact. It's not just a matter of how much money you save; a pallet project for the inside of your house can easily be a dominating graphic element, something that shows off your own particular design style. In fact, you should keep that in mind as you look through and consider the projects in this chapter. They are all easily modified to reflect a different aesthetic if you prefer. Mix up paint or finishing details, or go deeper and modify the actual dimensions or construction fine points to really create an original look.

In any case, the natural structural integrity of pallet wood will serve you well on anything you create for your home. From a plant tower to a clock, the wood is sure to hold its own over the long haul and be with you for this home and wherever you move to next.

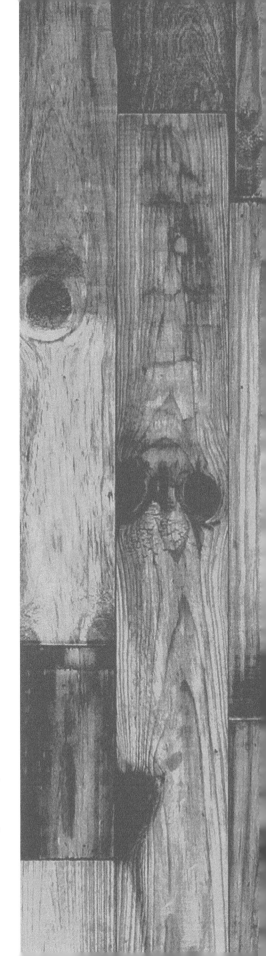

PLATFORM BED

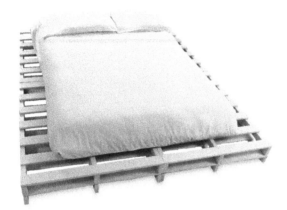

WHAT YOU'LL NEED

TOOLS:
Pry bar • Palm sander • Paintbrush (optional) • Hammer • Power drill and screw bits

MATERIALS:
8 pallets • 100-grit sandpaper • Primer (optional) • White gloss enamel paint (optional) • 3" wood screw • (14) 4" zinc mending plates and screws • 4" wood screws • Self-adhesive felt furniture pads

TIME: 1.5 HOURS   **DIFFICULTY:** EASY

A comfortable bed is one of life's great luxuries. Although we think of the mattress as the key to comfort, mattresses are just one part of the equation. The best beds provide a solid foundation that doesn't feel like it might collapse under you as you toss and turn during the night. The bed should also support the mattress in a way that will ensure the greatest longevity of the mattress, because mattresses are anything but cheap. Fortunately, you can save a nice little chunk of change with a pallet bed like the one in this project. You'd be hard-pressed to find a bed more secure and simple to construct than this platform.

The design of this bed is unconventional and lends a modern, almost industrial look to a bedroom (although the bed itself can be entirely concealed with oversized blankets or comforters). It's an exceedingly simple look that you can dress up in a number of ways, from painting the pallets to siding them with a custom-made fabric "skirt."

No matter what you think of the look, though, there's no disputing that the construction of this project is perfect for the amazingly popular proliferation of memory foam mattresses. Unlike box spring sets that require only side rails for support, memory foam mattresses

call for a firm foundation with closely spaced slats. The gaps between slats allow for air circulation that will help combat mildew and dust mites, and a platform bed like this eliminates annoying squeaks and sounds common to rail frames and less sturdy slatted beds.

The design in this project is sized to accommodate a standard queen-size mattress, although it can support a king-size unit if you're willing to give up some of the border space on the platform. A smaller double or twin mattress will look lost on the platform though.

One of the wonderful things about this bed is that it's so easy to assemble. Because the bed sits flat on the floor, it is relatively self-leveling, and there are no precise measurements to take in the fabrication process. You also won't need any special skills or tools. You can make the process even easier by nailing, rather than screwing, the pallets together (just use more nails). As a bonus, it's almost risk-free. If you find that the bed isn't to your liking, it can easily be deconstructed and the pallets reused in another project.

PICKING THE RIGHT MATTRESS

The beauty of a platform bed like this is that you don't need a box spring, which potentially saves you a good bit of money. However, depending on the type of mattress you select, you can easily eat up that savings. Manufacturers are increasingly offering hybrids, such as mattresses that pair an innerspring core with a memory foam top, but the market is still dominated by sales of the individual types listed here.

● **INNERSPRING.** This is the traditional mattress, usually paired with a box spring that is mounted on a traditional metal rail frame. But the mattress will last just as long and perform just as well on the slatted surface of a pallet platform bed like the one in this project. Quality among innerspring mattresses varies wildly. A bare unit with minimal padding over the spring core will cost little more than $100 and can be expected to be comfortable for five years at most. A luxury "pillow-top" mattress with thick padding and a heavy-duty frame may carry a twenty-year warranty and a price tag close to $1,000. There are a wealth of options in between.

● **FOAM.** The most recent innovation in mattress technology, memory foam units continue to grow in popularity. The thickness and type of foam (most companies use proprietary formulas) determine comfort, longevity, and price. At the high end of the spectrum, these mattresses can run thousands of dollars and offer a premium sleep experience. But even at the budget end, these miracles of modern technology offer sleep comfort most people find superior. Foam mattresses are ideal for a pallet platform bed because the technology actually requires the mattress be placed on a slatted surface with gaps, rather than a solid platform. The weight also ensures that the mattress moves around on the platform less than an innerspring or air mattress would.

● **AIR.** Air mattresses can be adjusted to suit your preferred firmness, and they are the least expensive among the options listed here. However, they are also the least comfortable and tend to make noises as you move during sleep. They are the least desirable option because they are prone to movement and the pallet platform bed in this project doesn't include channels or fences to hold a mattress in place.

● **FUTON.** A time-tested type of simple mattress formed of layers of batting surrounded by a durable canvas body, futons are an acquired taste. The surface is softer than a floor, but harder than any other mattress type. Futons are relatively inexpensive and, because of their simple construction, can last decades. Used on a pallet platform bed, they raise the top level of the bed only a couple of inches, so if you choose a futon, be sure the bed as you've built it is at the height you prefer.

You don't necessarily need to build a base layer for the platform bed to get it to a comfortable height. This home crafter created a top layer of four pallets and strategically placed wood bolsters underneath as a foundation that allows for increased air circulation and easier cleaning under the bed.

This simple twin-size bed was formed by nailing unfinished pallets together to form one long, narrow surface. The futon mattress is tough enough to withstand the occasional splinter, and the bed took little effort and only a few minutes to make. This is the perfect space-efficient, dorm-room bedding solution.

HOW YOU MAKE IT

1. Remove the bottom deck boards from eight standard pallets. Smooth the pallets all over with a palm sander so that no rough spots or splinters remain.

2. If you're painting the bed, prime and paint the pallets all over. You can paint them any color, but white is the most common and the least likely to go out of style. If you don't like white, gray or very pale blue or green would work for most bedrooms.

3. Set four pallets in a grid, laying upside-down on the top deck boards, with the stringers running from what will be the foot of the bed to the head (notched edges up). Fasten the two pallets together, side by side at the head of the bed, with 3" wood screws. Drive screws every few inches, alternating sides.

4. Repeat the process with the two pallets at the foot of the bed. Fasten the stringers of the foot pallets to the head pallet stringers with 4" zinc mending plates screwed to both sides of each stringer pair. Reinforce the connection by screwing mending plates at the center point of the deck boards (on the underside) across the pallets.

5. Build the base layer on top of the first layer, notched edge up, with the remaining four pallets fastened in exactly the same way.

6. Alternating sides, drive 4" wood screws down through the stringers of the top layer, into the stringers of the layer below. Attach self-adhesive felt furniture pads every 3" along the bottom of each top stringer.

7. Use a helper to flip the bed and position it in its final location. Check for any splinters or rough spots before sitting the mattress on top of the bed frame.

POTTED PLANT TOWER

A sturdy storage structure for potted plants is the type of small feature that many homeowners overlook. That's unfortunate, because often the condensation, occasional spills, and modest dirt associated with any collection of potted indoor plants can ruin a bookshelf, a counter, or even a floor. A nice potted plant display center like this one can show off your plants to their best advantage and keep them from marring other surfaces in the home.

The interesting stairstep design was developed to ensure maximum sunlight exposure for the plants you place on the tower. Even large, leafy plants won't shade out the specimens on the lower shelves.

That said, this doesn't necessarily have to be placed indoors. The very nature of pallet wood ensures that this can go on a patio, a deck, or even out in a garden; it will endure whatever the elements throw at it and stay in great shape. Decorated properly, it could be a lovely addition to any outdoor sitting area and will help you exploit limited available space for a full-fledged container garden. You can even leave one half of the structure free for occasional overflow seating.

Finish the construction as you like and in the best way that suits the interior or exterior of your home. Placed inside, it will look nicest painted. You can consider it a chance to play around with dynamic contrasting or complementary colors. Paint different levels in

WHAT YOU'LL NEED

TOOLS:
Pry bar or pallet buster • Frameless hacksaw or reciprocating saw • Circular saw • Measuring tape • Carpenter's pencil • Power drill and bits • Palm sander • Paintbrush (optional)

MATERIALS:
2 pallets • 4" wood screws • 2" wood screws • 80-grit sandpaper • Paint or finish (optional)

TIME: 40 MINUTES   **DIFFICULTY:** EASY

different shades of the same color or in a jumble of hues. Or go wild and paint all the different pieces in their own colors. Of course, you can also play it a bit safer by finishing it in a pleasing dark stain—just add a top coat of clear polyurethane to ensure that the occasional drip doesn't ruin the wood.

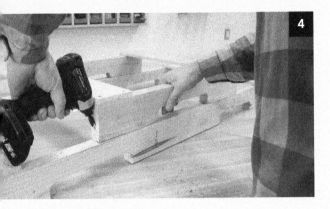

HOW YOU MAKE IT

1. Using a pry bar and frameless hacksaw, remove all but the end boards on the top of one pallet and all the bottom boards. With a circular saw, cut the remaining boards along one edge of the center stringer. Remove all the bottom boards from a second pallet, and cut the top boards along the center stringer.

2. Cut two sections from the second two-stringer pallet. One will be 10" long, ideally with the deck board centered along the length; the second will be 24" long, ideally with deck boards on either end, 3" to 4" in from the end (remove any boards between the two outer boards). Note: You may have to remove and reposition deck boards on the longer stringer to accommodate the design.

3. Measure and mark one of the removed deck boards into two sections, each 10 ½" long, then cut.

4. Set the middle 24" section on top of the base, centered end to end. Toe-screw it in place with 4" wood screws. Set the top section in place on the middle section, and fasten it in place in the same way.

5. Measure and cut six deck boards to fit over the ends of the stringers for each level. Fasten the deck boards in place on the ends with 2" wood screws.

6. Sand the structure all over and paint or finish it in your desired colors or tones.

FIVE EASY INDOOR PLANTS

There are dozens of houseplants you can display on your plant tower, but these five are some of the best in terms of how easy they are to care for, how widely available they are, and how interesting their growth is.

● **ASPARAGUS FERN:** A distinctive look for any indoor garden, the asparagus fern will do fine in full sun or in a shady part of the room. The fuzzy fronds like consistently moist soil.

● **CHINESE EVERGREEN:** This simple plant offers large, light green leaves with attractive beige stripes. It likes full sun and will tolerate the occasional overwatering.

● **PRAYER PLANTS:** Want a dark, dramatic foliage display? Look no further, because this plant grows oblong leaves with painterly patterns in purple, pink, and red on a dark green background. It does best in stippled light and with modest watering.

● **PHILODENDRON:** With an astounding number of varieties from which to choose, the philodendron is naturally one of the most popular houseplants. Its shiny green leaves feature cutouts that make them look like someone has taken scissors to them. A weekly watering and shady location will be ideal for a healthy philodendron.

● **SPIDER PLANT:** This is a favorite in homes coast to coast, because it is easy to care for and knife-like fronds with a white center stripe add drama to the home's interior. Give it sun and water once a week and it will be happy.

PLAY STRUCTURES

Every so often, pallet seekers come across a treasure trove. It can be a dumpster overflowing with pallets that a construction company makes clear they aren't going to reclaim or recycle. Or maybe a local discount store goes out of business, leaving behind an untidy tower of old pallets they are just hoping goes away. Wherever they come from, when you salvage a large quantity of pallets, you take what you get. There may be some mismatched sizes, and several of the pallets may be slightly (or more than slightly) damaged. Whatever the case, reclaiming a large number of pallets is equal parts work and reward. All of the pallets will require a thorough cleaning before use, and you'll want to sand or otherwise treat defects and areas that might lead to splinters.

You can use the pallets for any of the projects in this book or others of your own design, but a large collection of pallets begs to be used for something that will benefit specifically from the abundance. A yard or play structure is ideal, because it can be built from unmodified pallets and can be designed to use up a large inventory.

Using pallets for building structures makes sense. There is natural strength and durability in the structure of the pallets, because the deck boards are usually attached to the stringers or blocks with incredibly strong fasteners. The downside is that, when left in their original form, the pallets have gaps in their surfaces. There are many ways to deal with that issue. In some cases, as with a playhouse that will only be used during the day and in good weather, the gaps simply don't matter. If you're hoping to use the structure in inclement weather, or just want a truly enclosed space, you can cut and rip deck boards to fill in the spaces on the pallets you're using, or staple plastic sheeting or another barrier on the inside walls and ceiling of the structure.

The bigger challenge is the design of the structure you want to build. Using pallets whole to build any kind of a structure requires careful planning. You should draft a design on grid paper, measuring the pallets to ensure everything fits as planned. Then, it's just a matter of executing the design for the structure you want to build.

● **PLAYHOUSES.** Start with the foundation. Clear a space slightly larger than the footprint of the playhouse. Dig down a couple inches, if you're okay with the foundation sitting above ground level. Otherwise, excavate six inches and lay down a one-inch layer of gravel; the top of the foundation will be roughly level with the surrounding ground. Create the foundation by screwing stringers together with four-inch deck screws. Use more screws than you think you need to ensure the integrity of the foundation. Single pallets can be used for the walls and can be screwed directly to the foundation by laying pallets stringer facedown and screwing the walls in place. In most cases, a flat roof will do just fine.

Although a pallet playhouse won't look as finished as the units offered at retail, there are advantages over prefab playhouses and more involved playhouse plans. A crude structure such as this allows kids to use their imaginations to pretend the structure is whatever they want it to be—from a castle to a three-bedroom bungalow.

The rough-and-tumble nature of the structure is perfect for play. Children can mark up, beat on, or just abuse the structure all they want without worrying about being punished. They can use it as a chance to express themselves with crayons, paint, or other materials that wouldn't be welcome inside the house or in a more formal, prefab playhouse.

● **TREEHOUSES.** The base is key in any elevated structure, and no more so than in a treehouse. The challenge is to design the treehouse to accommodate an existing tree. Keep in mind that the closer the house is to the ground, the safer it is. But in any case, the most stable platform for a treehouse is one that is supported by the crotch formed between the trunk and a branch or branches. To ensure absolute stability, fasten base pallets to one another and to the tree. It's wise to use lag screws or similar fasteners, because there's no such thing as overkill when constructing a treehouse base. You'll also want to check for level several times as you work.

You can use the base as a simple platform to enjoy quiet time in the tree, but in most cases it makes more sense to construct at least rudimentary walls to ensure nobody falls off the platform. Craft a more involved structure for youngsters who want an elevated clubhouse, but keep in mind that safety is key. Walls should be kept low. If you're going to construct taller walls, it's wise to sandwich pallets, creating strong, double-thick walls. However, any structure you create in a tree also has to be as lightweight as possible.

To enclose the walls or the ceiling, use the thinnest exterior plywood you can find and clad the outside of the structure in the plywood sheets.

QUICK 3

Some pallet creations bridge the gap between furniture, structure, and safety feature. These divide or connect spaces and can actually serve vital roles. The three options included here not only define the space in a home; they are also simple projects to construct because they use pallets whole or relatively whole. Each of these features a simple design that won't require much in the way of fabrication skill, effort, or expensive tools to assemble. All are innovative applications that can be used purely for function or spruced up as decorative architectural elements. Just keep in mind that these are all related to home safety, so it's imperative that you be careful when constructing and installing them to ensure they don't cause harm where they were meant to ensure against it.

....

1. CHILD'S SAFETY GATE

Safety gates are essential to keep toddlers corralled and to prevent them from venturing up or down stairs, or careening around a busy kitchen. But plastic gates can be pricey and look, well, slightly cheesy. Create your own safety gate by cutting the deck boards along one edge of the pallet, and then cut the two-stringer section to match the opening you need to secure. This process is a simple one that only requires careful measuring. That said, you'll also need to smooth the surface of the cut pallet all over to ensure that there is no area on which a child could get a splinter or cut themselves. Finish the gate as you prefer (consider a fun primary color design to amuse the little one). To complete the gate, screw sturdy hinges onto the stringer ends at one side, and fasten a gate latch tongue (one half of the gate latch) to the opposite end of one stringer. Position the gate in the space where you need it, check for level and mounting height, and mark for the gate latch receiver. Screw the hinges to one side of the opening and the receiver to the opposite side. Test the gate's operation and make adjustments as necessary.

2. FIREPLACE SURROUND

Although you can use this technique for a handsome and unique fireplace surround, the same procedure can be used to create a one-of-a-kind accent wall, a backsplash, or even a decoration for the base of a kitchen island. The idea remains the same: screw vertical battens in place to which the boards are attached with finish nails. The trick is in the planning and working out the math. Rip and cut pallet deck boards to the length and width of a subway tile to create an incredibly cool look in a kitchen, or leave the boards whole for a more rustic appeal. Either way, they should be sanded and cleaned up prior to use for the best final appearance. Around a fireplace, you'll need to be careful to keep the edges of the surround as far as possible from the firebox, to avoid any possibility of fire. Within those parameters, you'll find an amazing number of possible designs. Rip the boards to a skinny width and run the battens horizontally to build a dynamic wall surface that has all the visual motion of rain. Or really go detailed and arrange the boards in a herringbone pattern for an arresting visual accent wall in your living room.

3. ROOM DIVIDER SCREEN

Pallets make excellent room dividers because they visually separate different areas while still allowing for air and light penetration. Build individual walls for the divider by setting a pallet on a stringer face and then screwing a second pallet on top of the first (if you just want a knee-wall divider, you won't need the top pallet). Connect successive divider sections with three-inch marine hinges attached to the stringer ends. Use large, round, self-adhesive furniture pads under each wall to prevent the stringers from scratching floors. Using this method will take less than an hour to construct a bifold or trifold screen. Be aware that the screen will be heavier than most room dividers, and you should enlist the assistance of a helper in moving the screen. The real fun in this project is decorating the divider. You can simply sand, prep, and paint a pallet divider in color schemes to complement or contrast your decor. For even more flair, staple fabric panels over one or both sides of the walls to create a true privacy screen. Stencil or screen images onto the deck boards to make the screen a focal point of any room, or use it as a display wall for a group of framed photos or even for a favorite piece of framed art.

FIREWOOD HOLDER

A fireplace or wood-burning stove is an absolute luxury, especially during colder months. Even a firepit can be a special feature in your landscape, one that can serve as a social center at least three seasons of the year. All of those, however, require a good supply of dry, seasoned firewood.

Dry is key. If your wood gets soaking wet, it's going to steam and smoke as much as it burns. That can make for an unpleasant experience sitting by the fire or trying to heat a room with a wood-burning stove. That's where this simple, rudimentary structure comes in. The whole purpose of this project is to get firewood off the ground and keep it as dry as possible.

In addition to protecting wood from wet weather, providing good air circulation all around and keeping wood off the ground can also limit the insects and other critters that might make your wood pile home. Those can include black widow spiders and snakes, so this secondary goal is no small issue. Of course, on a more superficial level, a firewood holder keeps the wood stack tidier and looking neater.

Be aware that this project requires a lot of pallets and a lot of time. Dedicate the better part of a weekend to getting it right, because it will be very unsightly if left unfinished.

The actual construction isn't super challenging. The holder was designed to incorporate pallets or pallet sections in as nearly original form as possible. That limits the amount of deconstruction work you need to do, but also creates some fabrication challenges. The way the structure is built does not necessarily follow best standards and practices because it doesn't need to. It's a little odd to toe-screw members together, but it will work. In addition, you can add metal mending plates and corner braces to reinforce the construction anywhere you think necessary.

Finishing the firewood holder in any way is kind of beside the point. This is meant as purely functional construction. Get the measurements right and align members during construction and the piece will be as handsome as you could hope.

HOW YOU MAKE IT

1. With a pry bar and frameless hacksaw, remove the bottom deck boards from all of the pallets. Remove the top deck board at one end of four pallets. Choose and level the site for the firewood holder and lay down a bed of sand or gravel. *Note: It's easiest to build this project on location, because the finished project will be heavy and cumbersome.*

2. Cut down the four pallets on which the end board was removed by sawing along the center stringer, leaving four two-stringer sections. Strip the waste portions of the deck boards off two of the waste stringers.

3. Place two of the two-stringer sections on a flat, level surface, upside down (resting on their deck boards). Butt the stringer ends of both sections end to end to make one long base. (Butt them on the ends opposite where the end board was removed.)

4. Center a waste stringer along the inside face of the butted pallet stringers on one side. Ensure that it is flush with the stringers, and use 3" deck screws to screw it to the pallet-section stringers. Repeat with a second waste stringer on the opposite side.

5. Measure and mark one stringer of a remaining two-stringer section 3½" down from the end (on the end from which the deck board was removed). Cut that stringer. Repeat with the last two-stringer section, measuring and cutting the opposite stringer on the second section.

6. Use scrap 2x4s to temporarily brace one of the cut two-stringer sections standing—with the cut stringer at the top—on one end of the base. The vertical stringers should be flush with the base stringers. Check for plumb and screw the vertical stringers to the base stringers toenail fashion, using 4" deck screws. Repeat the process at the opposite end of the base, with the last two-stringer section. (The cut stringers for the two end sections should be on the same side of the base.)

7. Use a pocket hole jig to drill two pocket holes at both ends of each 2 x 4" x 8' pine boards. Screw one across   the uncut stringer of the two end sections, flush with the top of the stringers. Screw it in place with 3" deck screws.

8. Measure and mark the distance between the inside of the cut stringers on both sides (it should be 89"). Cut the second 2 x 4" x 8' to that length. Toe-screw the 2x4 into place between the two vertical cut stringers, flush with the tops of the stringers. Use 3" deck screws. This is the back of the unit.

9. Place one of the remaining whole pallets standing on end, centered between the inside edge of the sidewall stringer edge and the base butt joint. The bottom should be flush with the bottom of the base stringer. Drive 3" deck screws through the rear 2x4 header and the base's stringer into the back pallet stringer edges. Repeat the process on the opposite end with the second whole pallet.

10

11

10. Measure and mark with a Sharpie for 26" sections along the length of the corrugated plastic roofing panel. Cut the marked lines with a jigsaw equipped with a carbide blade. Smooth the cut edges with an emery cloth.

11. Starting from one side, fasten the cut roofing panels in place so that the ridge valleys run front to back. The first panel should be aligned with the outside edge of the sidewall and centered front to back. Secure it in place with 1" fasteners, driven every 4" along the edge and the front and the back. Continue fastening the roof panels in place, overlapping the edges, until the roof is complete.

DESK

We all need a good, solid place to work. It doesn't matter if you have a home office or just do your work in a corner of the living room—you need a desk. The best desks are big enough to spread out, forgiving of the occasional meal or cup of coffee during a work session, and are admirably sturdy. All that pretty much describes the desk in this project.

One of the truly great things about this desk is its sheer durability. Although it's a nice enough design to fit right into a living room or other space of the home, it's also tough enough to be a workshop centerpiece—a place where you can draft brilliant plans for innovative pallet creations.

The design is actually streamlined, very neat and trim. But it does have a craftsman-style feel and will complement and work with many different types of decor styles.

You can stain or finish the desk as you prefer, but you might want to avoid painting it. A work surface like this looks rather odd when painted.

HOW YOU MAKE IT

1. Deconstruct two pallets. Cut eleven desktop boards and four aprons 20" long from deck boards. Sand them smooth all around.

2. Cut four legs 25 ¾" long and two cross braces 38 ½" long from stringers. (If your stringers have cutouts, buy and cut the legs from clear lumber such as poplar.)

3. Build the leg pairs by screwing each cross brace to the tops of two legs with 3" wood screws. The ends of the brace should be flush with the outside faces of the legs.

4. Place the desktop boards aligned on a flat, level work surface. Sit a leg pair upside down across the boards, on either end, and adjust the boards and the leg pairs so that they are all flush with the ends and edges of the cross braces. Drive 2" wood screws down through the cross brace and into the boards. Repeat the process with the second leg pair.

5. Screw the nine remaining desktop boards in place in the same way, butted tightly together between the two end boards, to complete the desk top.

6. Drill pilot holes and use finish nails to nail the upper side aprons in place, flush with the desktop boards.

7. Measure up from the bottom of the legs 10" and use a level to mark a line on their outside faces at that point. Align the top edge of each lower side apron with the marks, and fasten the aprons in place as you did the upper side aprons.

8. Measure to confirm the length of the front and back deck boards, with a flush overlap of the side aprons. Cut the front and back aprons from deck boards, and drill pilot holes to mount them. Nail them in place. Install the lower back apron in the same way.

9. Sand the desk all over and finish as desired.

FURNITURE LEGS

As handsome as this desk is, you can put your own signature style on it by forming the legs in a unique way. Legs are often the indicators of style for a desk, and this one is no exception.

● **LATHE TURNING.** Although you'll need both a lathe and the expertise to use it correctly, this is a quick way to modify the bottom sections of the desk legs to a uniform and attractive shape. Picking from a variety of shaping tools, you can add rings or shape the entire leg down to a point. Lathe turning is a great way to form a shape that incorporates the notch as an intentional design element—rather than leaving it as is and risking that it looks a bit accidental.

● **JIGSAW SHAPING.** Building on the notch to create a more complex profile in the leg is an ideal use of a jigsaw. However, you must be certain that you don't remove so much wood that you compromise the integrity of the leg. Something as simple as a series of small wedges cut out of the edge that includes the notch can make for a repetitive design element that really makes legs stand out. Carefully plan out any jigsaw designs, and transfer all the cuts to the leg with a carpenter's pencil at the same time. That will give you a chance to consider what the entire leg will look like once cut with the shapes.

● **SANDING.** Although it's a slower process that requires a bit more elbow grease, you can build on the shape of a notch in a stringer leg by rounding all the edges and corners, and even sanding undulations in the notched edge of the leg.

● **REPLACEMENTS.** If you find notches in stringer legs unappealing, or if you just think stringer legs are too blocky a look for your desk, you can opt for aftermarket legs. Cut the legs in this project off right at the bottom of the top surface aprons, and use the cut ends as mounting surfaces for metal hairpin legs (a mid-century modern look) or more conventional turned legs. You'll find these through online sources, and turned legs are widely available at home centers.

HANGING PICTURE FRAME

WHAT YOU'LL NEED

TOOLS:
Measuring tape • Carpenter's pencil • Speed square • Table saw • Bar clamps • Putty knife or sanding block • Hammer • Paintbrush

MATERIALS:
1 pallet • Wood glue • Finish nails • 80- to 100-grit sandpaper • Wood putty • Stain (optional) • 8 x 10" glass pane • Glazier points • Sawtooth frame hangers

TIME: 30 MINUTES **DIFFICULTY:** MEDIUM

A picture frame is one of the most useful things you can make from pallet wood. Even small picture frames are pricey, and this one is easy to make and almost free. The nicely mitered corners create a polished appearance that will have guests in your home wondering where you bought such a nice frame.

To make sure that appearance is as pleasing as possible, be careful in measuring and cutting the miters. Be precise and cut the miters with a fine-tooth blade. You might also want to add a hanger on a side and an end frame piece so that you can easily swap the picture for one with a different orientation in the future.

In any case, the frame is a good use of scraps left over from pallet projects. If you're reclaiming a lot of pallets, make sure you keep all the scraps to make frames of different sizes—they make wonderful gifts, and relatives will cherish a family picture inside a handmade frame.

Take as much time choosing a finish as you do crafting the frame. The finish affects not only the look of the frame, but also how the picture will be perceived. You can use a distressed look or just stain the frame to emphasize the wood. But painting the frame is often a wonderful option—black or white will allow the photo inside to grab the most attention.

HOW YOU MAKE IT

1. Measure and mark the center of two stringers 10 ¾" long for frame sides, and the center of two stringers 8 ¼" long. Mark 45° angles out from the ends of the marks on all boards to create the miters for the frame (the outside measurements will vary depending on the exact widths of your deck boards).

2. Miter the ends 45°. The interior edges should be 10 ¾" on the long frame pieces and 8 ¼" on the short sides.

3. Use a table saw to cut the rabbets on the inside edge of each frame piece. Make one pass at the outside edge of the rabbet and one for the bottom to remove the material for the rabbet. As an alternative, use a router table to cut the rabbets.

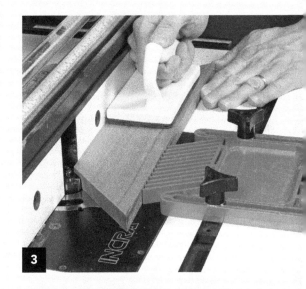

4. Glue the miter joints and clamp them with bar clamps. Drill pilot holes and nail the frame together through the miter joints with finish nails.

5. Scrape or sand off any glue squeeze-out from the joints. Putty over the nailheads and sand the putty smooth when dry. Distress the frame with gouges or other marks by sandwiching small sharp stones between the frame and a thick piece of cardboard, and shuffling your feet over the cardboard.

6. Stain the frame and let it dry.

7. Have an 8 x 10" piece of glass cut, and cut a piece of thin, stiff cardboard or poster board to match the glass dimensions. Lay the frame flat on its front, and set the glass into the rabbets. Lay the photo on top of the glass, put the cardboard or poster board on top of the photo, and secure the photo and glass in place by tapping a glazier point on each side of the cardboard back, into the edge of the rabbet.

8. Nail a sawtooth hanger centered on the top of the back of the frame (oriented according to the picture). Clean the front of the glass and hang the picture frame.

QUICK 3

The sturdy nature of pallets makes for wonderfully chunky and solid furnishings—especially if you're after a rustic look. But you can also manipulate the look of the wood with materials like glossy paint and glass to create interesting visual combinations or even transform the wood into a more sleek-looking material. The idea is that a piece of pallet furniture is adaptable; it can go modern or industrial, just as easily as it can fit a country-ranch interior. Whatever look you decide on, the truth is that the innate strength of intact pallets makes them a natural for use in furnishings that will be subjected to daily stresses. As anyone who has taken apart a pallet will attest, they are fastened together well to avoid falling apart under rough shipping conditions. Your living room can't begin to re-create the type of stresses pallets are made for.

1. COFFEE TABLE

Want an impressive focal point for your living room, one that takes less than twenty minutes of your time and suits all kinds of interior design styles? Look no further. A sleek coffee table is something almost every living room needs and can be a centerpiece that ties the room's look together. Remove all but the two end deck boards from the bottom of a stringer pallet and then clean up and lightly sand the pallet. Paint it high-gloss white (or another color, as you prefer) and screw four-inch casters to each bottom corner—including at least

one locking caster. You can leave the coffee table as is or give it a more polished appearance by having a glass top cut and edge-beveled for a solid top surface (a great idea if you happen to eat in front of the TV a lot or use your coffee table to hold small items such as remotes, iPods, or votive candles). Hold the top in place with self-adhesive rubber "dots," available at any hardware store or home center. If you don't have the room for a full-size pallet coffee table, or if you just prefer a more modest unit, you can cut the deck boards along the center stringer to create a more conventional rectangular coffee table that is two stringers wide. Follow the same steps you would with a full-size pallet coffee table.

2. MESSAGE BOARD

Every busy household should have a large message board to leave notes, make lists, or just jot down thoughts on the fly. It's a great household organization tool, but one that most homeowners never get around to buying, much less making. As with so many other projects, pallets can make this one easy. You can use a whole pallet if you have a large wall space and a very large, busy home. But most homes and families will be better served if you modify a pallet by removing the bottom deck boards and sawing the top boards along one end of the center stringer. The resulting two-stringer section will be your message board (cut the length down to fit available wall space or your own preferences). Sand, prime, and paint the stringers gloss white or a color that complements the wall where the board will be mounted. Prime the underside of the deck boards and paint with two coats of chalkboard paint. Mount the board into wall studs, screwing through the end deck boards. Tie a piece of chalk with string, and fasten the opposite end of the string to a screw in one of the message board stringers. Now you can jot down whatever important information you need to, and wipe the message board clean when it is no longer relevant.

3. BATHROOM MAGAZINE RACK

This is a super handy accent that usually is only considered when someone is using the bathroom. Magazines tend to wind up on the floor, get splashed from shower overspray, and generally clutter up the room. It doesn't have to be that way. It's a simple matter to create a basic magazine rack that will fit nicely with the decor of the room and hold all the magazines you might want to keep there. Cut two stringer sections twelve inches long. Cut four boards thirteen inches long. Screw one deck board section across one end of the stringer sections. This will be the bottom of the rack. Screw one deck board across the edges of the stringers, three inches up from the bottom. This will be the front. Screw a deck board across the opposite edges of the stringers, at the top (the end opposite the bottom). Screw a second board in place centered between that board and the bottom. Sand the entire rack all over with 80-grit, then 100-grit sandpaper. Prime and paint it bright white. Mount the rack on a wall near the toilet, driving a screw through each of the two back boards into a stud.

SIDE TABLE

WHAT YOU'LL NEED

TOOLS:
Circular saw • Pocket hole jig • Measuring tape • Speed square • Carpenter's pencil • Metal straightedge • Power drill and bits • Hammer • Palm sander • Paintbrush (optional)

MATERIALS:
1 pallet • 2 ½" pocket hole screws • Finish nails • 100-grit sandpaper • Paint or stain (optional)

TIME: 30 MINUTES **DIFFICULTY:** MEDIUM

Side tables are the forgotten players in living rooms, family rooms, and elsewhere. They are, however, wonderful and useful additions to the design of any room. They inevitably have a modest footprint that takes up little floor space, while still providing a top surface exactly where you need it for an accent lamp, a place to put a drink, or a resting ground for magazines or the TV remote.

Like all good side tables, this one has been designed for simplicity of construction and pure durability. The finished height is ideal for use alongside either a couch or a bed. It's also just the right size as a complement to a reading chair in a sunny corner of a room.

The design is handsome, but not so distinctive that it will clash with other furnishings. In fact, one of the key benefits of this particular table is that it blends so easily with most interior design styles. Whether you've put together a mid-century modern home or have opted for a more conventional traditional style, the table will look like a well-chosen member of your furniture ensemble.

The profile taper of the legs adds just the right amount of flair, and you can inject a personalized look by painting the table (complementary or contrasting colors in the top and base is an especially eye-catching look). But in most cases, finishing the table natural will be the more appealing look that works with the widest range of home styles.

HOW YOU MAKE IT

1. Cut four legs 20" long from stringers. Cut two braces 7" long and two braces 11" long from a stringer. Use a pocket hole jig to drill two pocket holes at either end of each brace.

Optional: If you have a planer or jointer, or a friend with that machinery, the final table will look much better and more polished if you plane and smooth the lumber before constructing the side table.

2. Measure 3" down from one end of a leg and use a speed square to mark a line at this point. Measure in 1 ¾" from an edge, along the opposite end of the leg, and mark this point at the end. (Adjust the length and angle of the taper as necessary to remove any notches or leave a portion of a notch as an interesting variation to a straight taper.) Repeat the process with all of the legs.

3. Use a straightedge to mark a line from the end mark to where the opposite mark intersects the edge of the leg. Repeat with the remaining legs, and cut them with a circular saw.

4. Cut four top boards 16" long from deck boards.

5. Construct the frame by screwing each short brace between the edges of two legs, with 2 ½" pocket hole screws. Connect the two leg pairs with long braces screwed to the inner faces of the legs. In both cases, the braces should be flush with the outside surfaces and tops of the legs.

6. Dry fit the top boards so that the overhang is exactly 1" all the way around. Mark the boards and the leg frame to key the positions of the top boards.

7. Starting from one side, lay a top board in position, key it to the marks, and drill pilot holes down into the braces and legs. Use finish nails to fasten the board to the leg frame. Repeat the process with the remaining boards.

8. Thoroughly sand the table all over, slightly rounding the ends and outside edges of the top boards. Prime and paint as desired, or finish with a stain or other product.

QUICK 3

It's easy to overlook the fact that deconstructed pallet wood can, when cleaned up, be quite handsome in its own right. Break a pallet down into its parts, and those parts can actually be decorative if used in the right way. Small home accents made with pallet wood can be lovely, especially when you put your own signature on them. These three projects are perfect examples. Not only are these creations interesting additions to any home (and incredibly useful, in the case of the key and scarf holder), but they also make unique and touching gifts. Of course, they can also serve as departure points for your own creativity. Build on these ideas to use up scraps or odd-sized pieces leftover from other pallet projects, and you'll be upcycling like a true pro. No matter how you adapt the projects, you're going to discover making accents like these takes an amazingly small amount of time and effort.

1. TEA LIGHT CANDLEHOLDERS

Pallet-wood creations don't need to be big to be impressive. These tea light candleholders are proof positive of that. Small and charming, they are simply sections of a stringer, cut at angles to make small "boat" shapes. A two-inch spade bit is used to drill a three-quarters-inch deep hole right in the center of each shape, in which a tea light candle can sit. Play with the shape as you like—square it off for a blocky appeal, or use a jigsaw to create a sexier, more curved profile. If you want a more substantial decorative feature, leave a stringer whole and round off the corners and edges with a palm sander. Then use the spade bit to make tea light cavities spaced evenly along the length of the stringer. No matter what type of candleholders you craft, you can finish them in a stain or natural finish, or go fun and fascinating with colored paints! Among the projects here, these are some of the most welcome gifts for birthdays, Christmas, and especially housewarming parties.

2. KEY AND SCARF HOLDER

Whether you have a front door entryway or a mudroom inside a busy back door, having a place to organize outwear and essentials such as keys and cell phones is one way to cut down on clutter and limit the particular frustration that comes from searching high and low for something you misplaced the minute you walked in the house. This key and scarf holder will be useful beyond containing just keys and scarves. Remove the bottom boards of a pallet and cut the top boards along one edge of the center stringer. Cut the resulting two-stringer section in half lengthwise. Cut a loose deck board to the width of the section and screw it across the ends at one end of the section (that will be the top shelf). Sand, prime, and paint the entire structure with a color or colors that complement the wall, entry hall, or mudroom where the storage feature will be hung. Screw it to two studs by driving screws through the deck board nearest the top shelf. Fasten hooks of various sizes—and in the styles that match your decor—to the underside of the deck boards, leaving enough space between hooks to accommodate hanging jackets, ball caps, and other outerwear.

3. BATHTUB CADDY

This is a simple luxury that will make your relaxing bath even more soothing. There is plenty of space on top of this caddy for votive candles, a magazine, a glass of wine, and even a loofah. Even better, it can be whipped together in about fifteen minutes, using scraps left over from other pallet projects. All you need are some basic tools and the desire to make the most of your bathtub "me time." This caddy is sized for the average tub width of thirty inches—it rests on the top edges of the tub sides. However, if you have a soaking tub or a spa tub in your bathroom, adjust the design to suit the different width. The principle will remain the same. Cut three deck boards twenty-nine and a half inches long, and two stringer leftovers ten and a half inches long. On a flat, level work surface, lay the three deck boards aligned in a column, long edge to long edge. Lay the stringer sections on their faces, across the boards on each end, three inches in from each end. Screw the stringer boards to the deck boards with two-inch wood screws. Sand the unit all over, being careful to smooth the entire surface (the bath is no place for splinters!), and then finish in a dark walnut-and-polyurethane combination product.

CLOCK

WHAT YOU'LL NEED

TOOLS:

Table saw or circular saw • 2 bar clamps • Palm sander • Measuring tape • Carpenter's pencil • Paintbrush (optional) • Woodworking compass • Power drill and bits • Jigsaw

MATERIALS:

1 pallet • Clock kit with motor and hands • Wood glue • 100-grit sandpaper • 1 ½" wood screws • Sawtooth frame hanger or similar

TIME: 20 MINUTES **DIFFICULTY:** EASY

This "timely" creation can be customized in ways limited only by your imagination and is incredibly simple to construct. Really, though, this project is as much about pure fun as it is about getting your hands dirty making something for the house.

Clocks serve both a decorative and functional purpose. That's why it's the rare room in the house that doesn't benefit from a wall-hung clock. Creating one like the clock in this project is an opportunity to design a fantastic accent piece that stands out as strongly as art would on the wall. A clock such as this also makes a wonderful housewarming gift.

Consider the basics of this project as a launching ground for your own aesthetic. Paint the clock face in vivid colors, choose a distinctive font to stencil for the numbers, or play around with the look of the clock to suit your own decor. Just keep in mind that you can go wild with a design accent this small because it should pop out, not blend into, the rest of the room.

The widespread availability of clock kits that include a battery-motor casing and two hands makes constructing the clock easy. The actual assembly process shown here won't challenge your DIY skills and certainly won't take more than part of a Saturday afternoon.

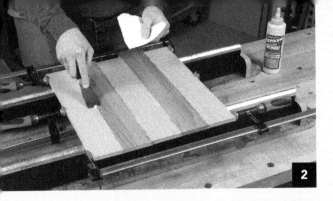

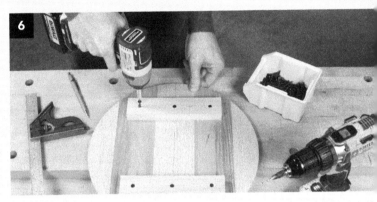

HOW YOU MAKE IT

1. Cut four 16"-long boards from deck boards; they must be free of serious flaws in the faces or edges. Check the post of the clock mechanism to ensure you can accommodate the thickness of your deck boards. (You can rip down boards as necessary and adjust the measurements to accommodate by adding boards or decreasing the finished size of the clock—it's 14" here.)

2. Edge glue the four boards together to create a 16" square. Clamp them with bar clamps until they're dry. When dry, scrape or sand off any glue squeeze-out. Sand the boards smooth for the appearance you're after (leave them rougher for a more rustic look).

3. Measure 7" down from one end, along the center joint between the inner two boards. Mark this point and wedge a brad or small nail in the joint at the mark. Use a woodworking compass to draw a 14" diameter circle on the face of the boards. Repeat the process on the opposite side of the boards.

4. Use a jigsaw to cut out the clock shape, following the marked circle on the front of the boards. Paint or finish the face of the clock as desired.

5. Rip and cut a scrap of deck board into two 9" x 1 ¾" cleats. Measure 2 ¼" down from the top of the clock circle drawn on the back of the boards and draw a horizontal reference line. Do the same from the bottom of the circle.

6. Align the cleats flush to the reference lines and centered across the circle. Screw each cleat to the clock boards, using one 1 ½" wood screw per board.

7. Drill a clock motor post hole where you secured the nail for the compass (the kit shown here requires a ¼" hole; size the hole according to the post for the kit you're using). Test fit the motor and the hands, then stencil or mark numbers on the clock face to correspond with the hand positions.

8. Nail a sawtooth hanger or other hanger onto the back of the top cleat and hang the clock.

DARTBOARD CASE

No self-respecting man cave can be called complete without a regulation dartboard. This one is incredibly similar to what you would find in a real, honest-to-goodness pub and will be a wonderful addition to the decor no matter where you put it.

It is meant to hold a standard, eighteen-inch-diameter board. The wood is an ideal backing because it stops the errant dart throw from putting holes in the wall.

The case is a handsome design and could just as easily be converted to accommodate a small group of collectibles or other storage needs.

It's all straight cuts and simple nailing or screwing, so there is nothing technically difficult about this project. In fact, you might even be able to put it together using scraps from other pallet projects.

WHAT YOU'LL NEED

TOOLS:
Pry bar or pallet buster • Frameless hacksaw or reciprocating saw • Measuring tape • Pencil • Circular saw • Power drill and bits • Hammer • Palm sander • Paintbrush (optional)

MATERIALS:
2 pallets • 3" wood screws • 2" finish nails • (4) 3" butt hinges • Gate hook and latch • 80-grit sandpaper • Paint or finish (optional) • 2" deck screws • Regulation dartboard and darts

CUT LIST:
(2) 1½ x 3½ x 21½" main frame rails • (4) 1½ x 3½ x 9¼" door rails • (6) 1½ x 3½ x 24½" stiles • (7) ¾ x 3½ x 24½" frame slats • (14) ¾ x 3½ x 12¼" door slats • (2) 1½ x 3½ x 4" dart blocks

TIME: 30 MINUTES **DIFFICULTY:** EASY

HOW YOU MAKE IT

1. Disassemble the pallets using a pry bar and frameless hacksaw. Measure, mark, and cut all the pieces to the lengths listed on the cut list with a circular saw. It's okay if some members include a notch, as long as cuts are made anywhere in the notch itself.

2. Screw a stile across the ends of two frame rails, and screw a second stile to the opposite ends to create the main box frame for the dartboard, using 3" wood screws.

3. Screw a stile across the ends of two door rails, and screw a second stile to the opposite ends to create a door frame. Repeat to complete the second door.

4. Lay the long deck board slats on the main frame, aligned edge to edge and with their ends aligned with the stiles. Make sure they are flush all around, and then drill pilot holes through each slat, into the stiles (and the rails, for the two end boards). Nail the boards to the frame with 2" finish nails.

5. Repeat the process with the two door frames, using the short deck board slats. Drill three ⅛" holes spaced evenly across the face of both dart blocks. Screw a block to a door rail in the corner between the rail and stile. Screw the second one into the second door, in the opposite corner.

6. Lay the main frame deck board-side down on a work surface, and set the doors in place, deck board-side up, on top of the frame (the dart blocks must be at the same end for both doors). Measure and mark for the hinges 3" in from the top and bottom of the doors.

7. Screw the hinge leaves to the main frame and doors on both sides. Screw the latch and latch hook to the deck-board side of the doors so that that the doors can be latched shut.

8. Sand the case all over and stain or finish as desired. Locate two studs in the mounting area. Mount the case by driving 2" screws through the frame slats into the studs at the top and bottom of the case. Use the supplied mounting hardware to mount the dartboard centered inside the main frame, and put the darts in the dart blocks.

OTTOMAN

This particular design is streamlined and pleasing to the eye, will take a lot of abuse and being bumped around, and is super comfortable thanks to a lushly padded and upholstered top surface.

The construction is basic and won't take you much time or expertise. If you've had to deconstruct a few pallets for another, larger project, you may even have the pieces you need on hand, ready for some minor modification and super simple fabrication.

Although the design has been developed to blend into as many different types of living room décors as possible, it also leaves a lot of room for you to put your own stamp of style on the piece. Instead of staining it, you could easily paint it in a single attractive color, or go bold with contrasting colors on the legs and the side and end boards. The fabric you use for the cushion will also make a big part of the style statement. In any case, though, a cleanable textile is best.

Ottomans can be the odd man out among living room suites, but anyone who has ever owned one knows just how nice they are to use. Not only is it a lovely little luxury to have a place next to your favorite easy chair to put your feet up and relax, but ottomans also provide extra seating that can be moved around and used as needed at events like large family gatherings. They can even hold plates of food or bowls of popcorn on family movie night, effectively serving as a second coffee table.

WHAT YOU'LL NEED

TOOLS:
Pry bar or pallet buster • Frameless hacksaw or reciprocating saw • Measuring tape • Metal straightedge • Pencil • Circular saw • Power drill and bits • Palm sander • Paintbrush or cloth • Staple gun and staples

MATERIALS:
1 pallet • ½" plywood • 2" wood screws • 80-grit sandpaper • Stain, finish, or primer and paint • Self-adhesive furniture pads • Spray fabric adhesive • Foam padding • Fabric

CUT LIST:
(1) ½ x 20 x 20" plywood cushion base • (4) 1½ x 3½ x 11½" legs • (4) ¾ x 3½ x 20¾" base end boards • (4) ¾ x 3½ x 22¾" base side boards • 3 x 20 x 20" foam padding • 23 x 23" fabric square

TIME: 30 MINUTES **DIFFICULTY:** EASY

1. Remove all of the bottom boards from a pallet using a pry bar and frameless hacksaw. Measure and mark the plywood cushion base to the dimensions listed on the cut list and cut with a circular saw.

2. Measure and mark two 11½" sections on the center and one outside stringer, with a deck board centered along the length of each section. Remove the other deck boards. Cut the deck boards along the outside edge of the center stringer, and cut the stringers at the marks.

3. Cut the deck boards according to the cut list.

4. Position one of the short deck boards across a two-stringer leg pair at one end. Measure and make key marks so that the board projects 1½" past the ends of the stringers and is flush side to side (this board should be on the same side of the stringers as the attached deck board). Drill pilot holes and screw the board to the stringers with 2" wood screws. Repeat with the opposite leg pair and second short deck board.

5. Join the two leg pairs by screwing one of the long deck boards across the outside faces of the stringers, overlapping the ends of the top board on both leg pairs. Screw a second board into position across the same stringer faces, overlapping the bottom board on the leg pair. Repeat with the remaining long deck boards on the opposite side of the leg pairs.

6. Sand the base frame all over with 80-grit sandpaper. Stain or finish it as you desire or prime and paint it in your preferred color. Stick self-adhesive furniture pads to the bottom of each leg.

7. Use fabric adhesive to stick the foam padding to the plywood base. Lay the fabric upside down on a clean, level work surface.

8. Set the cushion, foam-side down, in the center of the fabric. Carefully fold the fabric up over the edges, stapling it taut in place. Fold the corners neatly, and staple the foldover fabric to the base. Slip the cushion into the top of the ottoman.

PET BOWL HOLDER

dried dog food find their way outside the bowl. (And some cats aren't much neater.)

The pet bowl holder in this project helps prevent the mess in two ways. First, it stops the bowls from moving and sloshing as they do. Second, it raises the food dishes closer to the level of the dog's snout, which makes for a less messy chow time.

Thanks to the sturdy nature of pallet wood, the holder can be used indoors or out. You can finish or paint the base, but leave the top natural because your pet will probably be licking the top. Of course, it's usually easier to leave the whole structure natural, especially if it will be normally kept out of sight in a mudroom, utility space, or pantry.

You have to love your big, shaggy best friends . . . until they start to polish off dinner. Let's face it, dogs just aren't neat eaters. From the moment that tail starts wagging to seconds after all the food has been inhaled, a dog eating is a festival of mess. Water may be splashed across your floor, and errant pieces of

WHAT YOU'LL NEED

TOOLS:
Table saw or circular saw • Router • Dado blade set • Bar clamps • Carpenter's pencil • Woodworking compass • Power drill and bits • Jigsaw • Sanding block

MATERIALS:
1 pallet • Wood glue • 3" wood screws • Sandpaper • Pet bowls

TIME: 30 MINUTES **DIFFICULTY:** MEDIUM

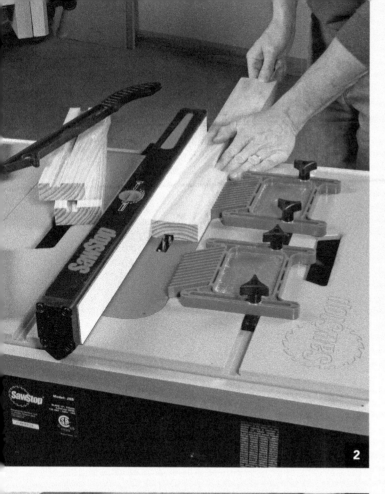

2

3

4

6

1. Cut two frame sides 21" long and two frame ends 9" long from stringers. Cut three top boards 19" long from deck boards.

2. Use a table saw equipped with a dado blade (or a router with a guide) to cut ¾" wide by ¼" deep dados in the faces of the frame pieces, 1" in from an edge (along the edge opposite any notches).

3. Edge glue and clamp the top boards aligned side to side. When dry, mark points on the surface 5" in from each end and centered side to side. Use a woodworking compass to scribe each bowl circle, centered around the marks.

4. Drill a starter hole in each circle, and use a jigsaw to cut out the circles.

5. Butt a frame end to the end of a frame side to create one corner (with the dados aligned and the notches facing down), and fasten them together with 3" wood screws. Repeat with the opposite frame end piece to create a U.

6. Slide the glued top into the dado slot. Slide the remaining frame side onto the top, and screw it to the frame ends on both sides. Sand to remove obvious blemishes and splinters, but don't finish the frame, because your pet will be licking it, so you'll need to avoid possibly toxic coatings.

EASY DADO DEPTHS

To quickly and easily determine how many dado blades you'll need to stack for a dado cut, set the wood that will go into the dado on its side on a flat, level work surface. Stack the blades up next to the wood to precisely match the height of the wood, and you've got exactly the dado stack you need.

METRIC CONVERSIONS

Metric Equivalent

Inches (in.)	1/64	1/32	1/25	1/16	1/8	1/4	3/8	2/5	1/2	5/8	3/4	7/8	1	2	3	4	5	6	7	8	9	10	11	12	36	39.4
Feet (ft.)																								1	3	3 1/12
Yards (yd.)																									1	1 1/12
Millimeters (mm)	0.40	0.79	1	1.59	3.18	6.35	9.53	10	12.7	15.9	19.1	22.2	25.4	50.8	76.2	101.6	127	152	178	203	229	254	279	305	914	1,000
Centimeters (cm)							0.95	1	1.27	1.59	1.91	2.22	2.54	5.08	7.62	10.16	12.7	15.2	17.8	20.3	22.9	25.4	27.9	30.5	91.4	100
Meters (m)																								.30	.91	1.00

Converting Measurements

TO CONVERT:	TO:	MULTIPLY BY:
Inches	Millimeters	25.4
Inches	Centimeters	2.54
Feet	Meters	0.305
Yards	Meters	0.914
Miles	Kilometers	1.609
Square inches	Square centimeters	6.45
Square feet	Square meters	0.093
Square yards	Square meters	0.836
Cubic inches	Cubic centimeters	16.4
Cubic feet	Cubic meters	0.0283
Cubic yards	Cubic meters	0.765
Pints (U.S.)	Liters	0.473 (Imp. 0.568)
Quarts (U.S.)	Liters	0.946 (Imp. 1.136)
Gallons (U.S.)	Liters	3.785 (Imp. 4.546)
Ounces	Grams	28.4
Pounds	Kilograms	0.454
Tons	Metric tons	0.907

TO CONVERT:	TO:	MULTIPLY BY:
Millimeters	Inches	0.039
Centimeters	Inches	0.394
Meters	Feet	3.28
Meters	Yards	1.09
Kilometers	Miles	0.621
Square centimeters	Square inches	0.155
Square meters	Square feet	10.8
Square meters	Square yards	1.2
Cubic centimeters	Cubic inches	0.061
Cubic meters	Cubic feet	35.3
Cubic meters	Cubic yards	1.31
Liters	Pints (U.S.)	2.114 (Imp. 1.76)
Liters	Quarts (U.S.)	1.057 (Imp. 0.88)
Liters	Gallons (U.S.)	0.264 (Imp. 0.22)
Grams	Ounces	0.035
Kilograms	Pounds	2.2
Metric tons	Tons	1.1

ABOUT THE AUTHOR

Chris Peterson is a freelance writer and editor based in the Pacific Northwest. He has written extensively on home improvement and general reference topics, including books in the Black & Decker Complete Guide series; *Building with Secondhand Stuff: How to Re-Claim, Re-Vamp, Re-Purpose & Re-Use Salvaged & Leftover Building Materials*; *Practical Projects for Self-Sufficiency: DIY Projects to Get Your Self-Reliant Lifestyle Started*; and *Manskills: How to Avoid Embarrassing Yourself and Impress Everyone Else*. When he's not writing or editing, Chris spends his time hiking, baking, and rooting for the New York Yankees.

RESOURCES

European Pallet Association (EPAL)

www.epal-pallets.org

National Wooden Pallet and Container Association

www.palletcentral.com

(703) 519-6104

Western Pallet Association

www.westernpallet.org

(360) 335-0208

INDEX

Printed in the USA
CPSIA information can be obtained
at www.ICGtesting.com
CBHW040529240424
7346CB00006B/6

9 780760 368596